The Diva's Guide To Drama

VOLUME 2
FRIENDS vs. FRIENEMIES

Neisha Robertson

The Diva's Guide To Drama

The Diva's Guide to Drama, Volume 2 Friends VS. Frienemies, Copyright © 2012, Dyneisha Robertson.

All rights reserved. Printed and bound in the United States of America. No part of this book may be reproduced or transmitted in any form without the written permission from the publisher. Published by Mink Ego Entertainment, LLC, Houston, TX;

Copyediting by Alexis Latshaw)

ISBN-13: 978-1481058896
ISBN-10: 1481058894

For more information regarding special discounts for bulk purchases of this book or to arrange a speaking event with the Author please contact AskNeisha@Gmail.com

Dedications

This book is dedicated to Sy'rai Amia. You are my best friend! I am so grateful that God saw fit to grant me you. You are the greatest example of God's Grace! I am so proud of the amazing person you are. I pray you always let your star shine bright! You're EXTRAordinary! You will do amazing things in this world!

May God go before you, set crooked places straight, and place you in the right places at the right times where you will choose to do the right things! May he grant all your heart's desires!

You are my life's Pride! I love you mommy's little Noodles! BFFs Always!

-Also-

This book is for every woman who ever said "Females can't be trusted".

Available NOW from Author Neisha Robertson

The Diva's Guide To Drama Volume 1 MEN

Get it today!

Dear Haters,

This book is about you. I know you are going to read this and you are going to get mad. You are going to become instantly defensive and offended by what is shared about you. But I want you to try something you have never tried before: being honest with yourself!

Listen, if you are honest with yourself while you read this no one will ever know but you. Instead of being mad that I revealed your ways simply say to yourself, "Yeah, I do that." Then forgive yourself and move on. You will never fix what you refuse to confront.

When you read this guide please make an effort to recognize that the only reason you are becoming upset is because you fear you will be revealed. Relax. I did not use names. No one can prove that this is you.

I know you are paranoid. Sometimes when you know the truth it feels like everyone on the outside can look at it and see your guilt. Believe me, that is mostly paranoia.

Do not be concerned that all arrows point to you. That's just paranoia trying to convince you that you've been exposed. Worse case scenario do what you do best: deny, deny, deny. Then follow it up quickly with what you do second best: defend, defend, defend!

I keep it 100%. I do not exaggerate. I do not twist the facts and I do not sugar coat. I simply tell it like it is!

Rest assured that I am not revealing your secrets in an effort to blast you. I am sharing it to reveal that no matter how strong a person is we all get caught slipping from time to time.. I will give it to you. You caught us slipping! Some of you more than once!

Now do yourself a favor and remember as you read this there is no need to be defensive. You did what you did. We'll forgive you. Now forgive yourself. It happened. It's over. And you do NOT have to be defined by your past!

Some of you are not bad people. Some of you have grown and do not continue to play an active role as a hater. That's wonderful. I hope this guide helps you stay free from your hater ways.

If anyone does confront you about your actions in the past let them know you have read this book and have indeed learned how to stop hating! Bam!

Your old friend,
Neisha

Preface

The Divas's Guide to Drama: Friends VS. FRIENEMIES is the second release of the series following Volume 1: MEN. I put together this brief guide in hopes that more women will learn the severe importance of keeping the squares out of your circle! Like its predecessor I kept this guide relatively short and to the point to encourage women to reference it frequently.

The idea for this book came to me after realizing how now, more than ever, foes are disguising themselves as friends. The wolves are hiding amongst our flocks in sheep's clothing.

There seems to be an overload of fake friends taking over today. Even more disappointing is the fact that most women either do not know how to recognize their secret haters or they do not know how to appropriately disconnect from these women without causing more drama.

With friends like yours who needs enemies? Remember the old adage "Keep your friends close and your enemies closer"? Well it is outdated advice. Why? Simply put, enemies have evolved a lot over the past decade. I am fairly young, however I can still recall a time when it was much simpler to determine who your enemies actually were.

Fifteen years ago, when I entered high school, I can recall very well who my friends were and who my enemies were. There was no guess work involved. It was common knowledge which girls I hung out with and talked to. It was also common knowledge who did not like me and who I did not like. This was all public information.

Nowadays this is not the case. At some point within the last decade Haters went mainstream! This is not to imply that Frienemies or Haters did not always exist. Since the beginning of time there has been documentation of both Frienemies and Haters. The Bible story about Judas is a prime example of this. Like most Frienemies Judas was a backstabber!

The world is full of Judases today. It takes a sick person to smile in your face and help plot your demise. No matter how deranged it is, it's happening every day. Hating is being perfected through the role of the Frienemy.

The line between friend and enemy has become severely blurred! To the untrained eye a frienemy is still a friend, but I challenge you in this book to look closer. Take a double take. Haters are taking a different stance today. They are playing a different role than before. There is none more dangerous than the enemy who poses as a friend.

How can you protect yourself from an unknown foe? Frienemies are much more of a lethal threat towards us than regular haters. This is mainly because they have the inside scoop. This gives them the upper hand. If and when drama pops off they have the advantage. They stay a few steps ahead every time.

This has become the cause of a surplus of drama. It has become exceptionally hard to determine who you can trust. I created this guide to show you how to reveal these so-called "friends" for who they really are!

I am going to show you how to point out who are your Friends and who is a Frienemy. We will start by defining the two in the first two chapters, entitled Frienemies and Friends.

Once you determine who they are you need to know what to do next. Inside these pages you will learn how to disassociate with them without causing an uproar of unnecessary drama during the process.

I encourage you to pray for Discernment from God. Ask him to reveal to you who is true and to protect you from those who are not. Wait for him to show you revelations in your relationships. Many people only do the first step; that is pointless. Make sure when you pray and ask for a sign you actually observe all the signs.

Too many people overlook the obvious signs of trouble. Just because you pray and ask God to show you your enemies doesn't mean that he will remove them for you too. We were created to live by our own will. Stop expecting to say a little prayer, wait for God to show you someone is untrue, and then wait for God to remove them from your life. No. You need to do the work. You need to be showing him that you observe and respect the signs by acting on them.

If you picked this book up I must assume you are at a minimum curious about your circle or friends. It's incredibly valuable for everyone to run their circle through the test to determine if they are indeed "Friend or Frienemy". Sometimes the biggest, most dangerous Frienemy is the one we least expect.

I encourage you to dig deep into every section of this book and use this information to calculate who is really real in your life. You may be surprised who passes and who fails. My definition of a friend is likely different from what you currently define a friend to be. As I elaborate on why I view things the way I do you will see my reasoning.

Inside you will also find the tricks to removing Frienemies without creating drama. The last thing any of us wants is to find out a friend isn't really a friend and then have to make a big mess in an effort to cut them off. I plan to show you ways around that.

I will also show you how to get over "trust issues", how to deal with the friends you outgrow and how to be the best friend to every friend you have.

Believe me when I say, it is no coincidence that you picked up this guide! In life there is really no such thing as coincidence. Coincidence is really God's way of putting something together. You could have stumbled upon any other book, but you didn't. You came across this book. Believe me when I say there is something inside these pages for you.

Be open to change. And have faith that there are good people lined up for your future. God is much kinder than we think. He doesn't want to see you alone, or with friends you can't trust. He wants you to have a support system of good people who are for you not against you. But first you need to remove the bad people. This book will show you who is against you and how to remove them from your life.

At the end of the day you can read this book over and over, but thoughts without works are pointless. I want you to take responsibility for yourself and not live with the fear that if you lose a bad friend you'll be alone with no friends.

As long as there is breath in your body you have the capability to make new friends. The world is packed with over 7 Billion people, chances are after reading this book you'll know how to find a few good friends!

That being said get ready for this book to show you how to create a life that is full of meaningful, happy, and trusting relationships. Get ready to develop relationships with women who are going places and encouraging you to come along!

Your future is full of people you can trust!

Your Friend,
Neisha

INTRODUCTION

My story

When I first wrote this Intro I filled it with the gritty stories of friends who turned into foes. Then I re-wrote it. I took a lot of the content out. I limited it to one story of betrayal per Frienemy. And then I re-wrote it again, and that is how we have arrived here.

My story is simple. Throughout my life I have always kept my number of friends to a minimum. I have never had five females that I called friends at the same time. A lot of people look at that as a negative, but I know that quite the opposite is true!

Friends are a lot like money: the more you have the more problems are going to follow. Unless, in both cases, you have so many/much because God gave them/it to you! I have never seen it work any other way. I have never seen a woman with six Un-Godly friends be able to hang around them all for long periods of time without some drama popping off about something. It's a recipe for disaster.

I have known successful and wealthy people. But I personally have never seen a person who earned their wealth in an Un-Godly way enjoy it without constant problems popping up everywhere they turn.

That is not to say that their problems are all financial. Generally that's the least of their problems if they really have wealth. But wealthy people who live life God-less seem to always have problems in other areas of their lives. They oftentimes have severe issues within their families. They are usually surrounded by Frienemies, in many instances knowingly.

However, when God places something in your life, whether it's friends or money, you can trust that it comes as a blessing. And the only person who can destroy your blessing is you! And the only way you can destroy a blessing is by missing it.

The reason I took most of the details out of this Intro was because I know the last thing you should do to a hater is give them any kind of shine! Writing my experiences would only trigger a reaction from them and that's the last thing I want to do. I have a strict policy that haters get no attention, positive or negative, from me. Never.

You see, that's what it is all about for them. They are insecure. Often they have no actual awareness of their own insecurity, but it is still true. It takes a person with low self-esteem to try and hurt someone they call a friend.

So, that being said, I deleted everything. These haters to get no shine on my watch.

Then I began writing. With each chapter I was reminded of the events in my life that took place. I was reminded of the betrayal and the hurt. That's when I realized I needed to share some of these stories.

Some of you who are reading this have not had severe incidents with haters (yet). Too many women under-estimate what lengths those you consider your friends will go to hurt you. I needed these women to see examples of how people change. Because people do change!

By no means have I always been a perfect friend. But you won't find a person who can tell you I did them foul. At most the only thing I'm guilty of is cutting these fools off abruptly with no explanation. I am notoriously good for that. You'll find a handful of my old friends who I figured out were indeed Frienemies who complain I just stop calling and stop taking their calls! I'll drop a hater like a bad habit without a moment's notice. I could not care less about it later. When it comes to cutting people off I can be cold-blooded!

I never slept with my friend's man, or ex-man. I never befriended my friend's ex just to gossip and tell him what she was *really doing* during the relationship. I never walked away from someone I considered a friend when they needed me the most. I never tried to wedge a gap between a friend and other people in her life (like her family). These things all happened to me, but I never returned the favor.

I don't know why people do the spiteful and unnecessary things they do when they do them. I am not sure what goes through their minds when they do what they do. But I have to assume that they justify it to themselves. I want to believe that they don't do foul stuff with the hardcore intent to be foul. But I don't know that for sure.

I can't imagine what goes through the mind of a jealous person because I don't get jealous. Why would I envy a woman who bleeds the same red blood as I do? Why should I be jealous of a woman who was created by the same God as I was?

Anything God has done for them he can do for me. I don't have a jealous bone in my body. Because I fully understand who created me. I know that I am fully equipped to run my own race. I could care less about being mad at another woman for crossing the finish line in hers.

Haters are the result of someone who wishes it were them and not you getting what you got. Frienemies are a result of a hater being jealous of a friend. The only people who get jealous are the ones who do not know their own worth…probably because they are too busy calculating someone else's.

Fortunately, I haven't experienced any extreme or tragic acts of betrayal by way of a friend turned Frienemy. I don't anticipate I will in the future because I am selective about who I let into my life now. However I have certainly witnessed some Frienemies first hand in the lives of people I know. I certainly could have been a victim of a tragic tale had I not always been so quit to cut a hater off!

I know a woman who found out her friend was pregnant by her man. I will never forget the scream I heard when I picked up that call. Frienemies are heartless.

I know a girl who had a so-called friend slashing her tires every couple of days, in the middle of the night. It was the biggest mystery for weeks. We couldn't figure out who was sneaking into her garage to cut her tires. Ah haaaaa…come to find out it was a Frienemy!! That was one of the most shocking and ruthless Frienemy attacks I've seen because we were all so shocked when we found out who it was. That's when I learned: it's never who you suspect in those situations. Frienemies are heartless.

Not all Frienemies go to these drastic extremes! As a matter of fact most of them don't. Mainly because, at the point you can reveal this type of betrayal, you undoubtedly already know to cut them off. However, we are going to focus on revealing the low-scale, deep-cover hater who lurks in the shadows doing petty stuff while waiting for the perfect opportunity to drop the hammer on you!

What's extra sad is sometimes what they consider a perfect opportunity is the precise moment something bad happens to you. They perk up when you call and vent your bad news. That's what haters are all about. They want you to be miserable like them. Misery loves company and I'm about to teach how to never go over for a visit!

Not all the friends I ever made were bad. I have been blessed with several great friends. Lifelong friends whom I can trust and depend on. Friends I can talk to in a judgment free zone. Friends I love and love me.

Life is about making sure you know the difference between the two as early as possible.

In my life I have been lied to on more times than a lot. I have been talked about. I have undoubtedly been judged. And I have been hurt. But one thing I can honestly say is that none of the above was able to keep me from my destiny! It's not from lack of trying, though.

It's a result of my being willing to cut ties with people who plot against me. Only the strong will survive. The weak will remain right where they are, complaining about how things never get better and nothing ever changes.

This book is all about the wonderful roles of friends and Frienemies. We'll begin with the latter because I feel once you know how to spot a Frienemy then you'll always know how to spot a friend.

The stories I share are 100% real! The people are all real Frienemies. I did not make these people or our story up! I do not sugarcoat or exaggerate my involvement. Everything happened the way I explain. I'm not all innocent, I have some guilt too! I have not always been a perfect friend, but I have NEVER been a Frienemy! Have I ever hurt a friend? Yes. But I have never had a friend come cut me off because I did something even remotely or slightly foul to them! [Comment: You don't need both "remotely" and "slightly", but it's not an error, just a suggestion.] Never!

You will certainly notice that the majority of these stories are between 10 and 15 years old. The reason being right before I had my first child I cut the B.S. out of my life! The older I get the fewer stories I have to tell. I reread this whole book after I finished writing it and realized that I only have one story that's within the last three years and it's the most mild story of them all. The reason being I nipped it in the bud before the drama began.

After reading this book you will learn how to forecast drama days, weeks, even months beforehand. There are always signs. I am going to teach you how to recognize them.

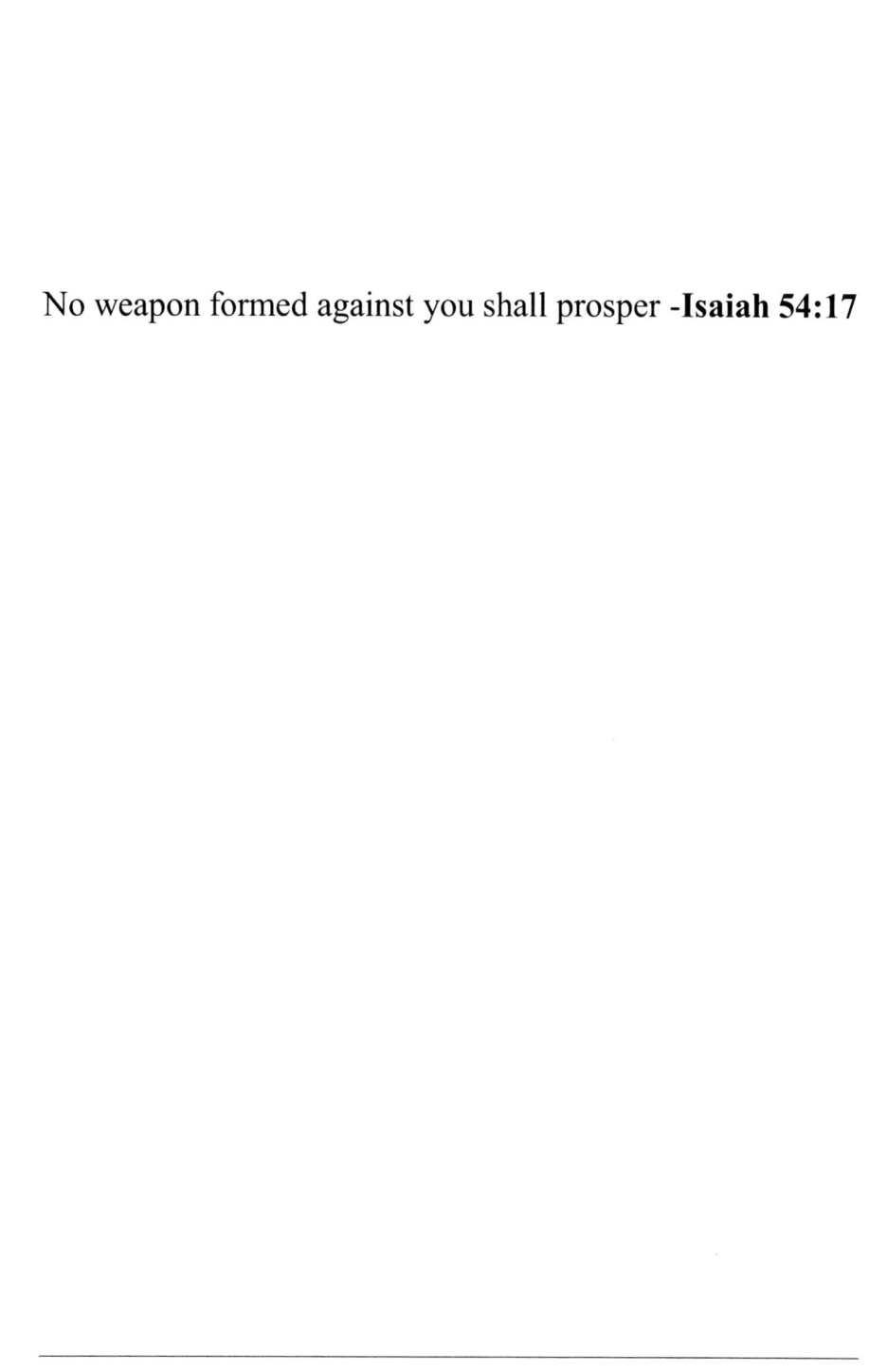

No weapon formed against you shall prosper -**Isaiah 54:17**

TABLE OF CONTENTS

Preface

Introduction

Chapter 1- Frienemies..27

Chapter 2- Friends..33

Chapter 3- Trust Issues...41

Chapter 4- When Good Friends Go Bad......................................48

Chapter 5- The Company You Keep..52

Chapter 6- Miss Narcissistic...65

Chapter 7- Fair-weather Friends...72

Chapter 8- The Jealous Ones..76

Chapter 9- Growing Apart..82

Chapter 10-Backstabbers..92

Chapter 11- Fighting in the Friend-zone....................................100

Chapter 12- Your Friends and Your Man..................................105

Chapter 13- Friends and Money...110.

Chapter 14- New Friends vs. Old Friends.................................116

Chapter 15- Goodbyes 119

Chapter 16- The Friend In You..128

CHAPTER 1

FRIENEMIES - HOW MANY OF US HAVE THEM?

When friends become enemies

What is a Frienemy?

Frienemy is a combination of the words Friend and Enemy. Why? Because that is precisely what a "Frienemy" is: an enemy posing as a friend.

Anyone can become a Frienemy. Yes, that means any friend you have currently! The majority of Frienemies begin as real friends. Most Frienemies didn't befriend you with the intent of becoming a hater. Jealously is what turns friends into Frienemies. Oftentimes even the Frienemy herself isn't conscious of the jealousy.

Jealousy is what turns friends into Frienemies.

Pathetically the jealousy is often unwarranted. For instance, most friends are on similar levels in life. How often do you see a successful lawyer whose best friend is a shampooer at a carwash? Rarely and almost never right? The reason is we befriend people who are similar to us in several ways, including success.

Therefore it is downright pathetic to be jealous of someone who is so similar to you, like a friend. But haters do it all the time.

Most Frienemies are jealous for very petty reasons. We live in an age where women are striving for attention; in some cases they are dying for it. This makes them absurdly competitive. So they become jealous of anything you have that gains the attention they desire.

Today women are so simplistic. Frienemies do not want much. All they want is everything you have. So they plot and pray for your downfall. They cannot stand the idea that you receive the attention that they want.

Everybody wants to be the star of the show. No one wants to just be the sidekick who supports the star. On the surface you may be saying to yourself, what attention? Why would anyone be mad at me for what I have? I don't have much. Well, it doesn't matter.

Sometimes it isn't the tangible things you have that they want. In certain cases it is your confidence they want, or your physical features. Some haters leech off your style, your persona, the way you think, walk, smell, laugh, they wish they could breathe like you or sleep like you, they are obsessed with the way you blink…these vultures want a piece of you. It can be the most obnoxious thing but they want it! And they begin to hate you for having it.

Don't waste your time trying to make logic out of why a hater hates.

There isn't usually a lot of rhyme or reason to it. It can be completely random and irrational. Don't waste your own time trying to make logic out of why a hater hates. You'll never figure it out. There's no sensibility to it. It's one of those times when you have to just accept the things you don't understand. Because there is no understanding the mind of a hater.

Accept the things you can't understand.

How to spot a Frienemy
There is no simple answer to explain how to spot a Frienemy. Different Frienemies do different things. However they all do things to reveal who they are. If you look closely you'll surely notice the signs. Simply put, Frienemies do the opposite of what real friends would do in the same situation.
In order to unveil a Frienemy you must make an acute effort to pay attention to what they do. Look for negatives in your interactions. Real friends are never negative.

Real friends are never negative.

Frienemies love to see you down
Listen for their response to your problems. Fake friends are quick to misguide you and even quicker to celebrate your problems. They may not be obvious or vocal in their delight, but they are often not vocal in their despair for your problem either.
Real friends feel your stress and become heavy hearted with trying to help you find solutions. Fake friends seem unmoved by things that move you.

Whenever a friend calls me with a problem my very first thought is what do *"WE"* do to fix this. I don't put myself at risk of allowing the problem to have a direct negative effect on my life, but I do feel responsible for being a part of the solution. I want to help my friend.

A real friend wants to be part of the solution. A fake friend is willing to stand by on the sidelines and watch you figure it out on your own.

You learn who your real friends are when you go through your most trying times in life. Real friends show up and help you make the "right" decision. Fake friends send you down the wrong path intentionally or vanish altogether.

Good friends always have a shoulder for you to cry on. Great friends dedicate themselves to helping you determine a positive solution to negative situations. Frienemies feel no connection whatsoever to your dilemma. They may extend a listening ear but they do not attempt to feel your pain.

When you call your friend with a problem and feel like they did not create a link between your problem's resolution and themselves, consider that friend a possible Frienemy. If a person doesn't care to help you when you have an issue then a person doesn't care about you.

The only exception to this rule is when you are a complete knucklehead who created the problem after you were warned of this exact outcome. Friends are not responsible for helping you with the unnecessary and easily avoidable messes you make. Friends should be there when you are a victim of circumstances that are beyond your control.

The more you know the more you grow

We will talk more in depth about the signs of a Frienemy in the later chapters. Please note that you must be open to change if you are really going to make a difference in your own life. You can't be resistant to removing these people from your life completely once you have determined they are indeed a Frienemy.

Keeping a Frienemy in your life is like keeping an enemy close, telling them your every move and all of your weaknesses and then standing still so they can attack and destroy you. It is never a good idea to forgive a Frienemy for being a hater and then letting them remain a part of your life. Forgive them, but forget them just as fast.

In all honestly you will read some truths that you will not like. You will learn that friends you least suspect are actually Frienemies. Be ready for that.

You will undoubtedly have to remove friends from your life that you like, maybe even love. It's sad but true. Get ready.

Life is all about people coming in and people going out. Sometimes people need to make their exit before we're ready for them to go. That's life.

Stop holding on! Stop clinging to people who are not benefiting your life. Let them go. Make them go. Make room for the right people to come in. Be strong enough to release the people who are not for you. Challenge yourself to be ready to do what's right as opposed to doing what you want. That's how you grow. You grow through what you go through.

Many times in life the right thing to do is the hardest thing to do. We absolutely have to do it anyway.

Stop clinging on to the people who are not benefiting your life!

CHAPTER 2

FRIENDS - THE ONES WE CAN DEPEND ON!

What's A Friend?

What is a Friend
     In order to fully understand what a Frienemy is you must have a clear comprehension of what a Friend is first.
     According to Google the word friend is defined as:

friend/frend/
Noun:
A person whom one knows and with whom one has a bond of mutual affection, typically exclusive of sexual or family relations.

     Now let's discuss that description. I want you to focus on these two words: "bond" and "mutual". The word bond indicates that there is a connection. The world mutual implies that two or more people share something in common.
     Therefore a friend is someone who shares a mutual bond with you. A friend is someone who is connected to you, not someone who feels disconnected from you.

A friend is someone who shares a mutual bond with you.

Friend or Foe

A friend is a friend all of the time. Friendship is a full time job. A person cannot be your friend one day, unfriend you the next day, and re-friend you two days later.

A friend should feel connected to what is going on in your life. A great time to survey a friendship is when you need advice or help. That's usually when Frienemies reveal their true colors. Deep down inside, Frienemies love to see you down. So when you ask for help up they usually pass on the opportunity to reach out their hand.

This is not to say that every mess you get into is the full responsibility and obligation of your friends. That is not true. No one should put themselves at risk for getting so deeply involved that the problem has an effect on their own life. That is not what I am saying.

What I am saying is that in every situation there is a way to give aid. Friends should always give you support and assistance with your problems. Sometimes the most they can do is offer you advice and words of encouragement. And in cases where that's all they can do to help you, should feel they are counseling you with passion. You should feel their desire to help through their words. You should feel their words come from the heart.

A good friend doesn't just listen to you and reply saying, "What are you gonna do?" There is more to it than that. Great friends want to get involved. They want to be a part of the solution. They are willing to extend their time and resources to help. They follow up with you to see how things are going. If things are not progressing well they stay committed. They don't get tired of your on-going problem. They don't help for a while and then, when they see things aren't getting better, stop because they are exhausted. Real friends never walk away. There is no opting out, real friends stay committed.

Real friends stay committed.

Real friends pray for you. They never get tired of helping you get through your issue. When you call they come running. That's what real friends do.

Fake friends have their limits. They may help a little, but they won't help a lot. It's not their problem. They validate this kind of thinking with the fact that they did not create the problem. They do not feel compelled to help you resolve it.

They are not committed to dedicating their time and resources to help you - especially over the course of time. They may help you with quick and simple problems, but the long term ones? That's out of the question. They have their own life to live. They can't keep interrupting their life for your issues. Not gonna happen. They have their own problems to deal with.

Fake friends have limits on what they are willing to do.

Lack of actions speak louder than words

Years ago I worked really far from home. I was a single mother with two very young kids and I struggled to make it financially. I literally lived check to check. I had no savings and at times my next check was spent before I even got it.

One day my car broke down. I needed to work more than ever to pay for the repairs, but I didn't have a way to get there. I had to lean on family and friends for rides to and from work. I felt guilty because the drive was always far for everybody. And to top it off I had to drop off and pick up my kids from daycare each way. I tried to spread myself around so I wasn't always asking the same people for rides.

Many times I would get a ride to work and not know who was going to be able to pick me up afterwards to take me home. It was one of these days I called one of my closest friends and asked if she would be willing to pick me up. I explained my sad story and apologized for even having to bother her, but I was desperate. She told me she had an appointment that afternoon to get her cd player put in at Best Buy.

That was at least five years ago. I have never forgotten the way that made me feel. I just could not believe that she was choosing a cd player over helping me. We were close. At least I thought we were. But apparently we weren't close enough to re-schedule that CD player appointment for a different day.

If I had known then what I know now I would have cut her off that same day. But I didn't. That is probably why I am full of stories where that same "friend" let me down. That exact same friend couldn't help me out on a different occasion because she was going to a movie.

I can't be certain, but I am going to guess that Best Buy would have let her reschedule for another day. But she didn't care if I walked home thirty miles in the dark. Her cd player came first. Sure, she could have caught a different showing of the movie, but why? Why would she miss out on plans to help me?

I understand that friends cannot always drop what is going on in their own life to accommodate me. I get that and you should get that, too. Friends are not liable for leaving work to help you or going broke to help you. Do not expect friends to cancel trips or miss important appointments. But expect friends to do everything they can every time they can. Recognize what things your friends consider to be more important than you.

What I do not get is how someone cannot weigh a friend as??more important that a cd player. I didn't get it then and I still don't get it now. I will never get that.

It's not as though she said, no, I have to take my daughter to the doctor. Or like she said, I am lying down and don't feel well. She said no I gotta get a cd player put in my car. And she had a clear understanding of the fact that I did not have many other options. But hey, it wasn't her problem. True story.

I do not have friends who mean less to me than installing a cd player, an IPod Aux. connection, or a radio. I am willing to re-arrange things that are not important to extend help to my friends. So if I am going to a hair appointment or picking out new tires for my car and a friend calls me for a ride, I'll choose to help my friend every time. As far as I am concerned everything else can wait.

On the tier of what is important in life, I list my family and my friends together at the top. Friends are family too. They are family we get to choose. I wouldn't leave my mother somewhere while I had a cd player installed, so why would I leave my friend?

Friends are the family that we get to choose.

When friends do not make you and your problems a priority then they are not good friends. Love yourself enough to see and recognize who is really for you and who is kind of for you sometimes, if they have don't already have plans. What are your friends showing you is more important than your relationship?

Love yourself enough to recognize who is *really* for you.

Why you need friends
I like to think of myself as an island. I have always been more comfortable being alone than most people. I do not know why, it is just my nature. I have never desired to have a lot of friends. I am the type who enjoys hanging out with the girls just as much as I enjoy chilling by myself. I like me so I think it is fun to just go out and grab a bite to eat by myself!

I like spending time alone. (Maybe a little too much). But I have learned that friends are a necessity. Friends are a must. We absolutely need friends.

For a long time I erroneously thought that there was no true need for friends. That is not true. We need friends to survive. Friends serve a great purpose in our lives. What we don't need is a lot of friends or Frienemies. We don't need any Frienemies.

We need Friends to survive.

I heard a saying somewhere, I have no idea where, that stated if you want to live go where the living are. We need to be around living people. We need to be around other people in order to stay alive.

Have you ever been depressed? Depression is a lonely disease. Think back on a time when you were depressed. Chances are you were either alone or with someone negative. Depression stems from isolation. Not being around people tends to drain your soul. People keep you charged, they keep you energized. And positive people keep you positive.

Positive people make you positive.

If you ever feel alone and have no one you can call on, go to a church and attend a service. Just being around people alone is fuel for your body. Churches are generally full of good positive energy. You absorb their positive energies and recharge. You don't even have to talk to anyone. Just being there is enough to refuel.

Friends give you life energy. When you are isolated you become dispirited. Look at prisoners for example. When prisoners are being punished, where do they send them…to isolation? Their punishment is separation from others. There is nothing more depressing than being alone. That is why we need people. We need friends.

Do not isolate yourself. Isolation leads right to depression. Why? It's simple; you were not created to be alone. You were designed to be surrounded by people. Find them! Find the good people who are designed to be a part of your life. They will bring you joy.

The better your friends are the better your spirits will be. If you are having a down day and you call up a good, positive, optimistic friend you will no doubt take on their energy! We need that. We need other people around us, giving us good energy and speaking good words over our lives. That is valuable.

We need friends for inspiration. You may not be aware of this, but your friends inspire your life. Our friends are our motivators. They are the ones who make us better - or worse. That is why it is crucial to choose good positive friends. Friends keep us alive. Friends help us thrive!

Friends inspire your life.

CHAPTER 3

TRUST ISSUES - WHO CAN YOU TRUST?

Good vs. Evil

Who can you trust

Most of us don't realize a friend is a Frienemy until after it's too late. Usually we don't see a Frienemy's true colors until the damage is already done. The problem is we trust too much. We trust people that haven't proven themselves to be trustworthy.

When you first meet a person you should consider everything they say to be questionable at best. People lie. And before you open your heart, home, or tell them your personal information, you should ensure that they are trustworthy.

Many people make the mistake of not stopping to ensure their current longtime friends are really trustworthy. It's never too late to find out. It's never too late to admit that you shouldn't trust someone because you have no verification that they can be trusted yet.

I have said it time and time again: put your trust in God…everyone else you meet you must thoroughly investigate! Everyone! That includes every living being with a pulse that you come in contact with on a regular basis. Never forget the saying, In God We Trust…everyone else we investigate!

In God we trust…everyone else investigate!

Understand that you can only trust people to the limit that you have verified them. You don't need to take chances on people. You cannot risk finding out the hard way that you trusted someone too much or too soon.

You need to take the time to thoroughly verify who your friend really is. You need to dig deep into how they treat other people in their life. Observe their relationships with their other friends. Do they take advantage of people? Are they constantly using others? Do they lie or steal from their friends or family?

In no way am I instructing you to feel privileged to judge others. You have no right to pass your judgment on anyone, guilty or innocent. But what I am saying is that you have a responsibility to verify who you let influence your life. And when it comes to new people I strongly advise you make few exceptions and take no chances.

If you determine that a friend is a Frienemy to others then they are going to become a Frienemy to you. You don't need to wait until you are a victim before you discontinue your friendship. Cut them off before they get the chance to victimize you!

What are people saying

Pay attention to what others are saying about this person. Sure, people lie about one another all the time. Not everything you hear about someone is accurate. However, do you really need to be the one who proves the rumors right?

If you can get enough separate and unrelated people to say the same thing about a person it's likely the truth. You can't always believe what you hear. But if five totally unrelated people tell you that the dog in the next room bites…assume that the dog in the next room bites. Don't go in there. Maybe they are all wrong. We may never know. But don't be the one set on finding out.

Investigate, Investigate, Investigate
When dealing with new people do a background check. Not the typical background check for violations of the law, I mean do a check of where this person has been and compare it to where they are right now.

When you meet a new friend find out who her old friends were. More importantly, find out who her current friends are.

I don't know any better way to judge someone than by the friends they hang with! This works in every way. I can determine who you are by looking at your friends. You can tell who a new friend is by looking at their friends.

Friends reveal everything about you. I can look at your friends and determine exactly who you are, and more importantly who you are going to be. You can look at your friends and determine the exact same thing.

Your friends determine who you are going to be.

Who can you trust

When determining if you can trust your friends, pay close attention to how they handle the responsibility of your friendship. Do they make you feel like a priority? How do they react when you tell them your problems? Figure out if they are dependable. When you make plans do they show up or is it always a gamble? Do they make a habit of canceling or rescheduling? Determine if you are a priority in their life. If not…assume they are a Frienemy.

Do they keep your secrets? Do they confide in you? A sure sign that someone isn't trustworthy is when they don't trust you. Learn to trust people a little bit at a time. Don't be so tempted to give all of yourself. You don't want to learn the hard way that a friend isn't trustworthy.

A good gauge on how much you can trust someone is how much they trust you with. Let them be first. Trust them on the levels that they show they trust you.

Most women trust too much too soon. Once you have investigated who a person is and confirmed that they are indeed a good friend then you should slowly relinquish your trust onto them. But you should always do so with the expectation that this person may prove to be untrustworthy.

Got Trust?

Just because people prove to be untrustworthy doesn't mean you should never trust anyone. You should be able to trust people. The world is overflowing with trustworthy people. If you don't see any, then look somewhere else.

You should be able to trust people.

Don't let the lack of trustworthy people in your past stop you from going out and befriending good friends. There are good friends out there who are not going to deceive you. They are not going to betray you and they are not going to take from your life; they are going to progressively add to it. They can be trusted.

Just like you wouldn't allow a bad ex to ruin all of your future relationships, do not allow a bad friend to ruin all of your future relationships. You should NOT be saying things like, "I've been burned/betrayed/stabbed in the back by friends before so I don't trust females." That's ignorant. Trust yourself enough to know that you are befriending better quality friends. Not every female is out to dog her friends. If you feel leery that women you meet have Frienemy potential then you are not meeting quality people. This is your own fault.

Got issues?

I can't count how often I hear women say they have trust issues. Whether it is with men or with friends women today always claim they can't trust. It's pathetic. Life has attached us all at one point or another, that's not an excuse to give up living altogether. Just because someone has proven to be untrustworthy isn't validation to stop trusting altogether. Move on. If everyone just stopped whenever we hit an unfair bump in the road no one would be going anywhere!

Please note if you have trust issues because you have been betrayed that is your own fault! You trusted someone who was untrustworthy. That was your bad judgment. Instead of going around complaining how men can't be trusted, or friends can't be trusted, you should be saying that "I" can't be trusted! The truth is you cannot trust yourself to make good decisions about who you can trust.

If you have trust issues that is your own fault.

I have zero issues with trusting people! Zilch! The reason why is I thoroughly investigate people before I trust them! And when I initially meet them I don't go all in and allow myself to be vulnerable. I trust a little bit at a time. I have no horror stories about people breaking my trust because I rarely release trust to the wrong people.

If you have trust issues that's your own fault. You need to do a better job picking your friends. If friends were close enough to you to betray you or break your trust, then you picked bad friends! You picked them! You trusted them! So it's all your fault!

The world is full of trustworthy people!

You shouldn't be going through life with trust issues! The world is full of trustworthy people! If the people you come in contact with are proving to be untrustworthy, then you need to find new people.

Do not dwell on the past and let the deceit of others be the reason why you can't trust again. That's worthless and insane. You need to work on trusting yourself. Learn to pick better people and then trust yourself to pick better people. Deeply investigate people before you give them your trust! If you have trust issues that only means you don't trust yourself. The real person you can't trust is you.

Do something

In order to break your cycle of befriending people who can't be trusted you need to accept the fact that you need to do things differently. You can't do what you have always done expecting a different result. That's insane.

Start to look into a person deeply. Find out their motives before you give them the opportunity to break your trust. Recognize that when a person steps outside the circle of trust they should not be allowed back in.

Put your trust in God. He will supply you with good people. Stop befriending the exact same type of women and complaining that all females are the same. No, the truth is all the females you become friends with are all the same. Break the cycle by finding friends who are different.

When you meet new friends, do not pour into them everything you have. Be modest. Give only a small piece of trust and see what they do with it. If they do well, give a slightly bigger piece of your trust, and so on. You shouldn't be trusting new people overnight. Expect the best, but give people time to prove themselves. When you do so you will discover that there are good people left in the world, people who will not betray your trust.

CHAPTER 4

WHEN GOOD FRIENDS GO BAD - THEY NEVER COME BACK

Loyalty is not an option!

Bad girls club

Loyalty is good until we find ourselves loyal to the wrong people. Like most people who enter our lives, friends can be seasonal. A sure sign that a friend is only seasonal is when they change for the worse. It is bound to happen from time to time.

Sometimes people are only supposed to be a part of your life for a certain amount time. God uses people to help you get to where he wants you to go. Sometimes, once that job is complete, the friend is not supposed to stay in your life anymore. A surefire sign it's time to evict a friend from your life is when they have made changes for the worse.

Numerous people make the mistake of trying to hold on to friends forever that are only supposed to be temporary! Nothing positive can come from keeping someone in your life after they are supposed to leave. Every time the result will be nonstop problems.

Whenever someone, anyone for that matter, is causing nonstop drama and problems in your life, take that as a definite sign that their season is up. Not everyone you are friends with now is supposed to remain your friend forever.

Look at your current friends. Believe that more likely than not some of them are seasonal. Get comfortable with the fact that the day will come when you will not know all of them anymore. It is going to happen and that is ok.

Whenever God takes anything from your life he always replaces it with something better. God is for us. He wants to be good to us. He isn't taking your friends away just so you have no one. He is removing people who no longer benefit you to replace them with people who will get you to your next level.

Whenever God takes anything he replaces it with something better.

When you have a friend that used to be really good and now it seems she has changed, recognize that her time is up. Once a good friend goes bad she isn't coming back. Not for you. When her season is up in your life accept it gladly. All that means is that you are moving into a new season. New people are moving your way. But you cannot move on to your new connections and new season when you are stuck in last season holding on to your old friend.

People come and go in our lives. We must be ready to move when it is time to go. If you are always trying to keep things the same, you are going to start moving backwards in life. By keeping things the same you have to remain in the same place. [Comment: I'd change this sentence to something like, "By keeping things the same, you are stuck in the same place."]

By God's design nothing ever stays the same. The only thing constant in life is change itself. You should expect that, however good or bad things are right now, your life will be different later. In order to ensure the future is bright, you must be willing to let go of old things. In order to get something new, you have to let go of something old.

Nothing ever stays the same.

She used to be so different

Not everyone changes for the better in life. I have seen many friends change for the worse. I have seen people I used to literally look up to switch from strong and determined to weak and victimized. I have seen women who valued their honor and self-respect turn into hoes. I have witnessed with my own eyes females who went from high standards to no standards. In life people change, and not always for the better, either.

In life people change and not always for the better.

It is mildly honorable to hold out hope that your once good friend will come to her senses and become good again. You should wish well for people. But do not hold out hope that things will change quickly enough for her new life to not have a negative effect on you.

When a good friend goes bad accept it for what it is. When she shows you that she isn't who she used to be, believe her. We lie to ourselves when we doubt our eyes. Believe what you see. She is who you see her as. Accept that and cut ties now.

When she shows you that she isn't who she used to be, believe her.

Once you see that the same friend is constantly causing trouble and drama, please recognize that as your sign that the friendship is over. By the time she is constantly stirring up drama in your life it was time for her to go a long time ago.

Live in the now

You can't base a friendship on the "used to be's". Do not live in the past with how great she was. Deal with who she is today. If she is a Frienemy today then she needs to be treated with the Frienemy response. She must be cut off. You cannot let her stay around based on the good deeds of yesterday. Her bad deeds today are all that matters now. Make peace with saying goodbye. Then move on without her. Don't look back.

CHAPTER 5

THE COMPANY YOU KEEP - WHAT DO YOUR FRIENDS SAY ABOUT YOU?

Why you are your sister's keeper

My Story

    I met this cute guy one night while walking to the bus stop after my after school job at a major department store my tenth grade year. He was a junior from a nearby school. He was kind enough to give me a ride home that night (I was 16 - I didn't understand the dangers of jumping in the car with strangers; I thought I was invincible).

    During our ride we talked about our lives. I found out he was a phenomenal young man for his age. He worked after school at a science lab where his mom also worked. He had saved his own money to buy his truck. He was an only child and his mother was very protective of him. And I could tell he'd been raised right.

Instantly we hit it off. His single mother worked like crazy so we'd often slide by his house after our weekend dates. He took me to his school dance. We were always going to the movies or out to eat. We hung out with his friends and he'd occasionally hang out with mine. Everything was fine. We got along great and had absolutely no drama.

Until one day when I was hanging out with my ghetto friend. She was cool. She had lived the rough life where she had been treated like an adult at a very young age and she was privy to seeing the nonstop drama boiling over in her life so often she'd become numb to it. At sixteen she had already seen more than most of us will see in a lifetime.

Her worldly ways didn't bother me, because it didn't affect the person she was on the inside. Deep down she was a good person with a big heart who had been robbed of her childhood. I probably shouldn't have been hanging around her, but how was I to know I'd be influenced in her presence?

So one day my good ghetto friend and I were bored like crazy. With little more than bus fare between us we didn't have many options for entertainment. I remember it was a Saturday night. I hadn't heard much from my boyfriend, which was a bit unusual but nothing major. She and I got the bright idea we were going to ride the city bus over to his house and see if he was home.

Unfortunately, the bus didn't travel very close to his apartment building. So we took the bus as close as we could get and walked a mile down to where he stayed. When we arrived we noticed his car was in the parking lot. Eagerly, I went to the security door and buzzed his apartment for entry.

Strangely, when he answered and I told him it was me, instead of buzzing me up he came rushing down the stairs. He was visually annoyed. He stuck his head out the door and asked why we had just stopped over unannounced.

I felt bad. It was a little embarrassing for him to react this way in front of my friend. After all, he was a good boyfriend and I had anticipated he was going to be excited we stopped by.

Nope. His mom was home. She usually worked weekends but he said she was home tonight and he could not have company over. He said we shouldn't have stopped by unannounced, and then he closed the door and went back upstairs. I was humiliated.

But before I could even say anything, she was like, "Nope, he's lying." I was confused. I realized she was upset even though he hadn't said two words to her. That's when she broke it down to me: he didn't want to let us up because he had another girl upstairs! She said it was obvious that he was cheating. I was shocked. I had lived such an uneventful and sheltered life I didn't even see the signs.

That's when she explained to me what I had to do next. She told me it was only right that he pay for what he was doing. So she took me to the parking lot and told me to key his car. I was so naïve. I felt weak that I didn't even know that this is how it goes down in these situations. It was slightly embarrassing.

Fortunately for me, my friend was willing to help me get up to speed. She gave me her keys. We walked around to the back of his old school Chevy Blazer and I began to make slices…unfortunately I lacked the experience and skill and my marks were barely even showing up.

She took the liberty to take matters into her own hands and carved my full name, Dyneisha, into the back of his Blazer, nice and big for everyone to see.

When she was done we headed back up towards the bus stop a mile away. We were barely blocks from his house when it began to unexpectedly pour down raining. We had no way to take shelter and not so much as hats to protect our hair.

By the time we made it up to the main street to the bus stop, we were startled to see my boyfriend's Blazer flying in our direction, going what seemed like a hundred miles an hour!

My heart was pounding out my chest. I was terrified. I didn't know what he was going to do. It was at that moment that I realized I was not about that life. My heart was beating in my throat. I figured he loved his car enough that he might put hands on us. It was dark and rainy and no one was around to help or save us.

I quickly glanced and my friend who was smirking ear to ear. She had that look on her face like I wish a mofo would! She was ready. Because, unlike me, she was really about that life!

He nearly jumped up on the curb. He left his window down and told us to get in the car. I didn't move. She hopped right in the back and he motioned for me to hurry up. Confused I hopped in.

It turned out he hadn't noticed the nice graffiti that she carved in the back of his truck yet. He just felt horrible knowing we were walking in the pouring hard rain and had snuck out to drive us home. He was sweet like that.

When we got downtown to my building my friend went inside and he and I stayed out in the car to talk. We had a good conversation. He explained his mother had grounded him and taken his phone for the weekend.

The more he talked the more I realized he was telling the truth. I didn't have the balls to tell him what we'd done to his car. I just played the happy innocent girlfriend role and prayed harder than ever that it wasn't going to actually show up. I was such a coward. I should have just told him so he wouldn't have to find out the hard way, but I didn't.

It was several days later when the shit hit the fan. In the meantime things between us were good. I used to work at a department store after school and he'd drive from his after school job at the lab to my job to pick me up. He didn't want his girlfriend to take the bus home late at night. Well this particular night I was stunned to see him standing outside his car angry with his hands folded.

Apparently his mother was driving behind him and panicked when she saw my name carved in the back of his car; she thought it was something gang-related. She freaked out. Naturally, when he saw it he knew it was me.

He was furious! I felt horrible. And like a true coward I instantly put all the blame on my friend. I figured it'd be an easy case to prove because she was left-handed and had very distinct penmanship. He didn't believe me.

No one believed me. He told my sister. She was furious with me. He told all of our now mutual friends what I did. They didn't believe me. I begged him to take me back. I begged him to believe that I really didn't do it. He told me even if she had done it, it was my friend and I brought her around and let her do it, so it was still all my fault.

Sometime later he forgave me. We have remained friends ever since, but we have never again dated. He couldn't get over it. He said he didn't know I was that kind of girl. I tried to tell him a hundred times that I wasn't, but he never believed me. To him I will always be just like my ghetto friend: ghetto. True story.

We like people who are like us

It is a proven fact that we choose friends that we view as similar to ourselves. That is how we make connections - our similarities. Our friends are people we have things in common with. We like people who are like us!

You are the company you keep

I have had women I know look me in the eye and defensively claim that they are not what their friends are. They swear they are not this or that. However I can see their friends are exactly what they deny being themselves.

I know grown women, right now, who believe they are sophisticated and classy, but their friends are on social media sites cussing out other women, threatening people, fighting, and snapping on their kids' father.

But even though her friends are clearly classless she claims that she is classy…it's just her friends that are hot ghetto messes! She's nothing like that. Yeah right! Get out of here with that! You are your friends. You can lie to yourself and say that it's not the truth, but that doesn't make it any less true!

You are who your friends are.

I wish more people would really understand that the truth doesn't need you to believe in it to make it real! The truth is the truth whether you accept it or not! The truth doesn't need you to be in agreement with it in order for it to be fact.

The truth does not need you to agree with it to make it fact.

So if your friends are a hot ghetto mess…guess what? You are a hot ghetto mess! If your friends are known liars, you are a liar. If your friend is a known whore, you are a hoe too. It sounds ugly, but it is what it is. We choose friends who are like us. When it comes to friendships, opposites do not attract. And, even if opposites did attract, which they do not, your friends heavily influence who you are. Therefore if you weren't like them initially you will begin to gravitate to being like them in time.

That being said, if you know your friends are haters, and you still maintain them as your friends, I have no option but to believe that you too are a hater.

The people you spend your time with are the people you get your inspiration from. Your friends give you advice - therefore they are your advisers. They counsel you when you are at a crossroad - therefore they are your counselors. With all of that being said, recognize that your friends play a real role in how you live your life.

So if your friends are seen as messy and always stirring up drama, then guess what people think of you? People see you as whatever your friends are. If your friends are unmotivated and lazy, I think it is fair to say the same is true about you. The people you surround yourself with are your representatives. Take a look at your friends and ask yourself, what do they say about you?

The people you surround yourself with are your representatives.

Do not get caught up in trying to deny this theory because you look at your friends and do not like what they represent. Remember, the truth does not need you to believe in it to make it true. What your friends represent represents who you are.

I know what you are saying to yourself. You want people to judge you for you and not for the people you associate with. The world does not work like that. When you and your friends go somewhere the world sees them and knows that you are the same. Instead of fighting the fact that you may have misrepresented yourself through the clique you chose, start to restructure your clique today.

In the meantime make peace with the fact that you and your friends are one and the same. If your friends are gangbangers…you are in their gang. If your friends are on the stroll, you may as well join them because to the world you too are a prostitute. It's a fact. You are who you hang around.

Frienemies are influential

Negative people are Frienemies. They may be descent friends on other levels however, if they are negative with the way they think or the way they live their lives, they are Frienemies all the same. The reason being is that they are influencing your life. You cannot live above the influence of those you surround yourself with. You will be what they are.

Life is precious. You cannot live a positive life surrounded by negative people. You cannot think positive thoughts if you are fellowshipping with negative thinkers. People rub off on you. You can make an effort to combat someone's negativity all you want, but in the end you will absorb whatever energy they give.

All of the people in your life mold the person you will become. There is no way around it. You are not the exception to this rule. Hang around negative people and you become negative. Therefore negative friends are Frienemies. They are the enemies of your positivity.

You cannot live a positive life surrounded by negative people.

My story

For over six years I worked for a large private company. For the first five years I worked in an entry level position. Everyone in my position was paid handsomely considering the job only required a high school diploma.

Along with a descent salary we received tons of money bonuses, free monthly lunches, free weekly massages, we could set our own schedules every week, we had the top of the line health and dental and had plenty of paid vacation days (around three weeks a year).

But even with all that everyone in the entry level complained. We were all dissatisfied. Most people with our education level and skill would have loved a job so comfortable and rewarding, but not us.

Every time managers came at us with a policy change or procedure update we scoffed. During breaks everyone sat around and talked about how much they didn't like this and didn't like that. We were all ungrateful. Everyone hated coming in to work. I was usually late and, even if I were on time, I always left early every day. I was making forty grand a year to do easy work and I too complained.

During my fifth year I applied for a management position and got it! I was barely given a raise. I was paid about two dollars more an hour to do a ton of more work. However, once I transferred into the managerial field, I was surrounded by professionals who viewed their jobs differently.

Instead of complaining about the increased workload everyone spoke positively about the great company (it really was great, all B.S. aside). Everyone pointed out how nice it was to have good benefits, good vacation pay, nice schedule flexibility, and a positive working environment.

Instantly I started to see it their way. The real truth was we had great jobs. Now instead of dreading coming to work I was getting there early and staying late! I loved what I was doing. I truly began to love my job.

Looking back, I realize that the manager's position wasn't better work. It was grueling work with higher expectations and barely more pay, but I was truly happy. I cried when I had to leave in order to move out of state. But that goes to show the difference that people make.

Negative people made me negative, even though I was in a positive situation. I should have been screaming for joy every day during that first five years. I had a manager I loved working with who favored me. My check was always correct and on time. What more did I expect?

But working around negative and ungrateful people influenced me to be negative and ungrateful.

Two types of people

I have discovered that there are two types of people in this world. There are people who think highly of themselves and their lives. And there are people who think lowly of themselves and their lives. When you meet new friends pay close attention to how a person speaks about themselves. Ask yourself, what does she think about herself? Is she positive? Is she negative?

People who speak negatively about themselves are just that…negative. They will speak negatively about you, too. Maybe not in front of your face (though some do), but they are negative people so you shouldn't expect a positive result from dealing with them. These are the people who see the glass half-empty. If they have a negative view of themselves, they can't be living a positive life.

Understand now that it is absolutely impossible to live a positive life full of positive experiences when you harbor negative thoughts. Not possible. So recognize that you don't need any negative friends! None.

It's a known fact: negative people are contagious. Stay around them long enough and you will surely catch it.

You can't live a positive life if you're full of negative thoughts!

Start over

No matter how you feel about it, the world is going to see you as the same or similar to your friends. Don't you want friends that represent your brand well? You should befriend people who you are proud to represent you in the world. When you look at the friends you have there should no shame, no embarrassment. You should see positive people who are current on their negativity vaccine.

If you cannot take pride in the fact that your friends represent you then you need to start over! You need to make new friends. Breaks ties with old friends. You need to be able to show your friends to the world proudly. Your friends should be an example of everything you want to be seen as. Especially since, not only do your friends represent who you are, but they influence who you will become.

Do not forget your friends are the same people whose counsel you seek when you come to a crossroads in life. You do not want to get your advice from someone who you don't want to represent you in the world. You want your inspiration to come from someone others view as wise and inspirational.

Feel obligated to find friends who are inspiring. Find yourself friends who are accomplishing their dreams and reaching new levels of success. If your friends are not motivating you to do great things you are selling yourself short.

Do not be afraid to start over. Find new friends. And this time be selective. The world is full of women who are great friends and great inspiration. If you search for them you will most certainly find them.

My suggestion is search for friends who are already successfully doing things that you want to do. There is nothing better than healthy competition between friends. Locate women who live the lifestyle that you want to be living!

Figure out what your dreams are. What you want to be doing. Then find friends who are actively doing it. Find some friends who are going where you want to go.

Don't feel obligated to be the leader. We have been taught to be the leader of the pack. I like to befriend people who can help lead me to new levels, as opposed to people I have to lead to my level. I'm already at my level. It's much more beneficial to befriend women who can show me a thing or two.

Aim for a balance. You aren't looking to be an apprentice, you're looking to be acquainted with people who you can learn from and who can also benefit from you. Good friends learn and grown from one another.

Show me your friends and I will show you your future! Whether you know it or not you will never be much more than your current friends are. We unconsciously strive to reach the levels that our friends are reaching for. If our friends are reaching new heights we reach with them.

Show me your friends and I will show you your future.

CHAPTER 6

MISS NARCISSISTIC

Miss It's All About ME!

Little miss narcissist

A narcissistic friend is a friend who is all about themself in an unhealthy way. Many narcissists are considered loners because they cannot find people worthy of being in their company. However, many of us have had narcissistic friends and some of you still have one.

In general, narcissism is described as being completely and utterly obsessed with one's self. These women are dangerously in love with themselves. Friends like this are a total headache to deal with!

Keep in mind that I am not a doctor. However, I have certainly had narcissistic friends; I know the traits. Your narcissistic friend is the girl who sees herself as more important and valuable than anyone else in the crew. She knows she is more beautiful, she flaunts the fact that she feels above everyone else, and she never wants to blend in with the group. She must stand out at all times.

What she needs from you

The narcissistic friends need constant praise from you and everyone else who wants to breathe in her presence! Because she needs you to give her praise she is very prone to exaggerating her accomplishments!

She must always have the spotlight wherever she goes. She can't operate unless she has the "special" treatment. As soon as the spotlight is on someone else she becomes an instant party pooper.

She is dependent on her friends always going along with her ideas. She has zero flexibility. If it's not her idea she will not be participating. Because no one has better ideas than her anyway! Especially considering her ideas always present her as the center of attention.

To say she takes advantage of others would be an understatement! She manipulates everyone in her life into doing whatever she wants. She has no empathy for anyone but herself. She can only be sympathetic when the sympathy is for her. But, even though she is not sensitive to the feelings of others, she is overly sensitive when it comes to her own fragile feeling.

There's only room on this pedestal for me

Do not waste your time struggling to maintain a friendship with a narcissist. Women like this will make you feel inferior if you are around them for too long. This is mainly because they literally view you as inferior to them.

Most narcissists are obsessed with their looks. And you could never be as pretty as she is (at least that's how she feels). Therefore she sees you as less than herself.

Narcissists have a lot of trouble maintaining healthy relationships/friendships. The combination of their selfishness, fragile self-esteem, and lack of sensitivity for others makes them targets for drama.

Case of the green eye?

I know that so many women are eager to attempt to confront troublemakers like Miss. Narcissistic. Do not bother. Narcissist have the same M.O. when you confront them, it doesn't matter what you are confronting them about. Every time you talk to them about anything they are doing wrong they will say that you are JEALOUS.

Narcissistic women are never guilty of doing anything wrong. Any and every attempt to accuse them of such is an obvious act of jealousy.

I am not sure what it is about narcissists, but they are always convinced that everyone is jealous of them. That's what makes them narcissistic. They have inflated egos! Be ready. Because there is a slim chance that you can talk to her about anything she is doing without her somehow viewing you as jealous. This ultimately leads her to disregarding whatever it is you are saying based on the grounds that you are simply jealous of her. In her mind everyone wants to be her.

Narcissists are convinced that everyone is jealous of them.

If you determine your friend is narcissistic you should stop being friends with her immediately. This is true for two reasons: A) She will view you as less than her and therefore treat you as such, and B) You do not need to spend your time stroking the ego of someone who never strokes yours back.

Give and Take

A good friend is supportive of you! A good friend lifts you up and makes you better. A narcissistic friend is not going to help you become a better anything.

You need friends who support YOU. However, do not become narcissistic yourself. You need to be a good friend, too. You should be supportive and uplifting with all of your friends. And all of your friends should support you, too. Good friendships are a two-way street. A friendship with a narcissist is a one-way street with no stopping any time. Do not waste your time. Do not cheer for anyone who doesn't cheer just as loudly for you!

My story

The most beautiful girl I have ever known became one of my best friends when I was around eighteen. She was drop dead gorgeous. I mean physically flawless. She bore a striking resemblance to Angel Lola Luv, except she had a much smaller waist and a much bigger butt (yes, I said a much better butt). Her body defied gravity. She was a brick house.

Don't get me wrong. A lot of young women who haven't begun having children have nice bodies. These days you can buy a small waist and a big butt. That wasn't what made her gorgeous. It was her face. She was a brown skinned bombshell. Men were always stopping in their tracks and having double-takes in awe of her beauty. She was like the black Kim K in our city. She was strikingly gorgeous! That's the only way to explain it.

She was a stripper- though she rarely worked because she didn't need to. She made in one night with one customer what most strippers danced for all week with tens of customers. She dressed up every single day. She wore minimal makeup, but what she did wear would be absolutely flawless. She was a certified dime.

The problem was she knew it all too well. Like most extremely beautiful women she couldn't keep a girlfriend or a man. That's a surefire sign that a woman is narcissistic, when she's physically flawless and cannot keep a man to save her life. And they usually can't keep many female friends either, because all of their friends become "jealous" of them.

Anyhow, we remained friends for years. Over the years I realized that everyone who knew her all agreed she was "special". There was nothing we could do about it. It was not hard to find someone who thought she was crazy. And you knew anyone who didn't think she was crazy just hadn't known her for very long.

She'd never respond to reasoning. She was never at fault for anything. And she strongly resented when people told her she was crazy - it had a way of making her crazier. So we stopped. We learned to just live with it. And by "we" I mean everyone she ever knew in life.

She wasn't a horrible person. She was a sweet girl, but she lived in a different world some days. All in all I brushed it aside and retained the friendship…until she unleashed her crazy on me.

If you read Volume 1 on Men in this series you are all too familiar with the story of my cheating, sex addicted first husband. (If you haven't read it you definitely should). Well, when I was pregnant with my son, my soon-to-be husband was cheating left and right! It was a nightmare. But, having recently lost my daughter's dad in a tragic and unforeseen crime spree, I didn't want to deliver another childless father, so I stayed.

I became distant and deeply depressed during my pregnancy. I cut off everyone I knew. I felt humiliated and embarrassed. I didn't want people to see what was really going on, so I withdrew. I stop answering everyone's phone calls and sort of disappeared.

My narcissistic friend, who was well aware of my fiancé's cheating ways, took my depression personally. She was very offended that I wasn't answering the phone. She'd leave crazy long rants on the voicemail of our house phone about how just because he was cheating was no excuse for me to take it out on her. I most likely would have called her back if it wasn't for her inappropriate tone, her nonstop calling, which was ignorant to stay the least, and her long ten-minute voicemail rants. It was so ignorant I really didn't know how to address it with her. So I didn't.

We lost years of friendship behind the fact that I became depressed about my man cheating on me. She made it all about her. She crossed the line several times in her messages. Her tone was always cross and she called back to back to back like I was her man or something.

We never regained our friendship. Had she been a normal friend I could have waited for the air to clear and sat down to have a rational conversation with her. But she was far from rational. To this day she still feels like she was the bigger victim than me with concerns to my Ex's cheating!

She's so vain she probably thinks this story is about her. True story.

CHAPTER 7

FAIR WEATHER FRIENDS - WHAT'S IN IT FOR THEM?

Can they stand the rain?

Seasonal positions

Everyone in the world will experience situations that are beyond their control. We all run the risk of being a victim. At some point we all experience down times. Every one of us needs a little help some time.

No one ever said your life would be easy. Life is full of constant change. Nothing ever stays the same. It is more likely than not you will experience seasons in your life where things change. Your life will have good seasons. Your life will unfortunately have bad seasons also.

The Good season

Good seasons are the seasons that are fun. The seasons when you have reasons to celebrate are the good seasons. They are the times when you rejoice because life is good!

During the good seasons people are easy to come by. It seems everyone is willing to help you celebrate when things are going well.

Everyone is willing to help you celebrate when life is going well.

It is not hard to find someone who wants to ride with you when you buy a new car. Everyone's your friend when your bank account is full. It's hard to choose who to bring when there's only so much room in the limo - everyone wants to come along. After you buy a bottle in V.I.P at the club, all of your girls want to join the toast.

That's what the good season is all about. Everybody wants to relish in your favor. People who barely know you are willing to help you celebrate and enjoy. Your friends are never too far or too busy to bask in the delight.

The good season feels like sunshine. It feels like perfect seventy-five degree weather. Love feels abundant. When things are going good you are never alone.

When things are good you are never alone.

The Bad season

The bad seasons are usually the exact opposite. They are the seasons that are comprised of tears, pain, and bad breaks. This is the season when you need other people the most.

When you lose your job it's hard to find someone willing to help you pay a bill. When your car breaks down it's damn near impossible to get someone to give you a ride. Once your refrigerator is empty you have a better chance getting groceries from strangers than the people who used to eat with you.

The bad season is often the loneliest season, as well. Most people do not want to help you with your problems when they are so busy trying to forget their own.

This is the season of storms. It's rainy, dark, and gloomy. It's the season when you stay in because it's bad outside. And it's the season when almost no one is willing to come over and help you weather the storm.

Almost no one is willing to help you weather the storm.

Granted, this isn't always true for everyone. Some of us have been blessed to find good people who stay the same in every season. However, most of us have had a few fair weather friends at some point.

Fair weather friends only come around when things are going well in your life.

Fair weather friends
Fair weather friends are the ones who are only around when things are going well in your life. They pop up to help have fun. They pop up when they have problems. But they disappear when you have to weather the storm in your own life.

They leech off what you have to offer. But they won't offer you a Kleenex when you're overwhelmed and at your breaking point...mainly because they are too busy leeching off someone who is having a good season instead.

People who are only around when the getting is good are Frienemies. If they can't help you at your worst they shouldn't be allowed to celebrate with you at your best!

People who are only around when "the getting is good" are FREINEMIES!

Pay attention

Be observant of who has time for you when things are not going your way. If you call your friend with your bad news, listen for her response. If she isn't vocal about helping you weather the storm, recognize that she is a Frienemy.

Fair weather friends serve zero purpose. They are users! They are not your friends. Friends shares a mutual bond with you. If she doesn't feel a bond to your storm then she is NOT a friend.

People only do what you allow them to

Take responsibility for the people you let enjoy the fruits of your labors. These women should not be partying with you when it's all good if they are not comforting you when it's all bad.

Real friends help you weather every storm. Real friends prove their dedication during your bad seasons. Next time things seem to be falling down around you take a look around. Be sure you notice who is there to help you pick up the pieces. Also be sure you notice who is not there. Anyone who is vacant during the storm needs to stay vacant when the seasons change. And the seasons always change!

Real friends help you weather every storm.

CHAPTER 8

THE JEALOUS ONES - A CASE OF THE GREEN EYE

They want what you have.

Envy

Jealousy is the biggest common denominator that Frienemies share. Most Frienemies do not even recognize why they are actually jealous, but they are all the same.

Many times there is something about themselves that they don't like, or even hate. And they envy you because of it. There is no rhyme or reason to their madness. Do not get wrapped up in trying to understand the reason why someone is the way they are. The "whys" rarely matter when it comes to haters. Especially in cases like this when none of it makes sense anyway.

The actual reason why people do what they do rarely matters.

We could look at a thousand different cases of the same type of hate and behind every single case there would be a different reason. The bottom line is: Frienemies are jealous. Why they are jealous doesn't even matter.

Maybe they don't want to see you shine because it makes them feel dull. It's possible they are hurt and they want to see you hurt. Maybe they never felt a mother's love and they hate that you have. Maybe they never had a relationship like you and your man have? Who knows! I mean the list could go on and on.

Instead of recognizing that life is unfair to all of us, they only focus on the fact that life has been unfair to them. In their eyes you should pay for that. They want what you have and they want you to have what they have. Really, it's a fair trade in their eyes. These women are pathetic.

They want what you have and they want you to have what they have.

Thoughts of a hater
What gives you the right to go around smiling and making the best of things? Who do you think you are breathing this free air like you're better than her? This is the type of foolishness that must be playing in the back of a hater's mind. Because in most cases they have no valid reason to be jealous - yet they still are!

Haters are the most super-silly people on planet Earth. We can guess what they are thinking, but we may never really know. They probably aren't thinking at all.

The bearer of Good News

Another bold difference between friends and Frienemies is how they respond when good things happen to you! Friends are eager to celebrate everything you do and every acknowledgement you receive. Friends love to see you be successful! They take honor in having a friend who is accomplished.

Real friends take honor in having a friend who is accomplished.

When you contact a friend with your good news they are ecstatic. Friends are the first to help you celebrate. They are enthusiastic about your news. They never make it about themselves. They are honored just to celebrate you. They see you as worthy of success.

Frienemies are often just the opposite. Frienemies take your good news as their bad news. They hate to see you get ahead. They downplay every victory. They never see your worth. Every time you get a step ahead in life it makes them feel that many steps behind you. They have a hard time celebrating your victories. Every time you find yourself set up for something good to happen, they take it as a personal setback.

Frienemies take your good news as their bad news.

Faking the funk

Many times Frienemies will pretend to participate in your celebrations, but it rarely feels sincere. They always have some excuse as to why they aren't giving their all to your celebration. The bottom line is you getting ahead is a threat to them. It's just one more notch in the belt of their shortcomings. It was bad enough when they had to compete with you before you got this breakthrough, now they have to climb that much farther to get ahead of you. It's a stressful time for a hater when you get a good break.

It's a stressful time for a hater when you get a good break.

Check yourself

Take heed of a person's response when you share your good news. And don't ever downplay the news of good things that come your way. Sometimes we feel like we are bragging when we share out victories. In an effort not to make someone feel bad we restrain from boasting about our good fortune. Never refrain from sharing your good news with a friend out of fear they will become jealous.

Whenever you hesitate to share your good news with someone out of fear they may feel bad about themselves, you are admitting that you realize they are a hater. The only time you feel concern about your good news making someone else feel bad is when you anticipate they will not take it well. That's a hater. Only a hater takes your good news as their bad news.

Haters take your good news as their bad news.

Friends never feel threatened by your blessing. A good friend knows that you are just like them. And whatever God does for you he can most certainly do for them. A good friend isn't so insecure that she needs to be first. A good friend is happy to see you win because she knows when you win we all win.

Friends never feel threatened by your blessing.

Evil wickedness
Jealousy can make people do some crazy things! Frienemies are all about destroying you. They usually take advantage of the fact that they are deep cover and stick it to you on the sly.

Once someone has gotten to the level of jealousy that creates in them a vengeful and evil spirit it's too late for you. There is no stopping the evil and wicked Frienemy once she is already in action. This is exactly why I urge you to identify your haters now and cut them off immediately. You can never be too early, but you can definitely be too late.

Keep it real with yourself
      Do not waste your own time hoping and praying that someone will change. You will undoubtedly have to cut ties with people you love and care about because they are not for you! If someone is not for you now, then they are against you forever. Don't bother trying to wait her out. Get her out, out of your life! Be honest with yourself. It is what it is.

Do not waste your own time hoping and praying that someone will change.

Empty thoughts
      When you go inside of the mind of the hater all you get is confused. These people make no sense. They are all just lost souls not even trying to find their way. Instead of working on improving themselves, they are more focused on being mad at you because you don't have their problem. It is a waste of your time to try to determine what's wrong with these kinds of people. We all have issues, but most of us don't choose to take them out on our friends. Instead of trying to determine why someone is jealous, accept that they are and cut them off!

CHAPTER 9

GROWING APART - WHEN THINGS JUST AIN'T THE SAME

The friends you outgrow.

My story

When I was homeless at fifteen there were a handful of nights I literally had no place to go. I thank God that there was never a night I had to actually sleep outside! However, there were a handful of times I had to "pretend" to be paying a friend a visit and then "accidentally" fall asleep.

I had a friend who, like me, was free to come and go however she pleased. Unlike me, she wasn't parentless or homeless. She just had a mother who let her run around like a grown women because she was too busy in the streets to actually be a mother herself. So we roamed the streets together. We "hung out" all night long. And on those few nights when I had no place to go she would sneak me in to her house to spend the night.

Technically there wasn't much sneaking involved. Her mom was almost never home, and the nights she did come home it was well after midnight and we'd already be asleep.

That was convenient until their family became homeless and had to move in with a relative. That's when I realized what a truly good friend I had in her. One night, when I had no place to go, she called her mom from a payphone (it was 1998) and explained my situation. Unfortunately, unlike herself, her mom did not feel obligated to my situation. Her mother told her I could not come over and she better come home immediately. That's when I heard my friend use a tone I wouldn't dare use with my own mother. She told her mom that she was NOT going to leave me out there on the streets and she slammed the phone down.

That's what friends do! (Not disrespect their mothers.) Friends feel connected to your problem. Friends love you. And they treat you like someone they love. And, just like every other form of love, they show you their love through their actions, not just their words.

I can't remember where we slept that night, but I know for sure I never slept outside so we must have figured something out. More than likely she called some friend who also had loose parents and they let us spend the night. Or maybe we slept over at a boyfriend's or something. Who knows? We teenage grown-ups; there's no telling where we ended up.

Fortunately, not long after that my older sister got her own apartment and I went to stay with her. It was such a relief not having to stress about where I would be sleeping every night. This allowed me and my friend to spend more time kicking it and less time stressing.

Even though no one was taking care of us we took good care of ourselves - at least physically. With no jobs and no money staying cute was a chore. But since we had no other chores (like most girls our age did) we embraced the task.

She turned me on to shoplifting. I was the most naïve, sheltered goober at fifteen. I never knew anyone who shoplifted. So imagine my surprise the first few times we left the mall, window shopping I assumed, and she pulled out a few new outfits! I was intrigued. I wanted in. So she taught me the ropes.

We would take the bus out to the mall. We walked around grabbing big stacks of clothes. Back then there was a store called Mervyns, it was similar to Burlington Coat Factory, and we would go in there and rack up! Once we get a real large stack of clothes we would head right to the dressing room. The dressing rooms were never manned by anyone. We'd go in the dressing room, pick a few (2 or 3) outfits we liked, put them on under our clothes and walk back out with the remaining stack and put it down like we didn't like anything. Then we'd nonchalantly walk right out. (Don't be an idiot and try any of this.)

One night when we were walking out I realized we were being followed by a man and a woman in plain clothes. And sure enough, just before we reached the door, they stopped us. Turns out they were store security. Apparently the signs in the dressing room that said they were monitoring were real. Even more real was the clause that stated shoplifters would be prosecuted!

We didn't go to jail, but we did have to go to court. I remember the police called my sister. She was only three years older than me, but she didn't play. It was a quick ride home on the bus that night. Why is it when you are a kid headed home to get in trouble time flies?

Since it was my first offense the judge gave me a year probation. The judge agreed to erase it from my record so long as I did not get a same or similar charge within that year. Thank God I didn't! I remember my probation officer would do surprise visits to my school frequently. I'd lie and tell people, say, social worker to keep people out of my business.

The whole incident scared me straight! I never stole anything ever again! I'm so blessed that I was a minor and that incident did not cause me to have a criminal record! I was scared straight from that day on! I do not even pick up loose change on the street. I'll be damned if I'm ever charged with stealing anything ever again. I've been called a lot of things since then, but never a thief.

My friend, on the other hand, stole plenty after that incident. Her mother didn't trip when she got home because her mother was a booster. Her mother taught her to steal. Hell, she was just working the family business!

If my daughter had a friend like this I would no-doubt advise her not to hang out with that friend! But I do not judge my friend. She was never taught anything more. And, though I believe that at a certain age we all know right from wrong, I think people who were raised without an internal guilt gauge deserve a slight pass. They never learned to do better.

This particular friend and I stayed close for many years until she moved out of state and we lost touch. Then we ran into each other about three years ago at a lounge. We disrupted everyone's evening that night. We were hugging and screaming it had been years since we'd seen one another. Naturally we exchanged numbers and the very next day she brought her kids by to meet my kids and we caught up.

During our catch-up session I found out her mother was serving time in prison for stealing and she had just recently been released from jail for theft herself. I realized then that she was almost thirty years old and still doing the same things we did at fifteen.

I was way different. In the ten years since I had seen her I had gone through a lot. The most important of which was the birth of my daughter and son.

My responsibility to my children as their mother was more important than any of my own needs. Since May 12th 2004, the day I became a mother, I have tried to walk the line as far as the law is concerned. I have seen too many cases, like hers, where mothers weren't being mothers. I know way too many people who grew up with a mother who was in the streets or in jail. I have seen that hurt and I know that it is real! I was not going to be that mother. I was going to be my mother. My mother was a woman who was always home being a mother first and foremost.

So, even though I will always and forever have love for my good friend, the same friend who loved me enough to sleep on a bus stop if she had to, I had to cut her off completely. It isn't about me judging her, because I don't know her plight in life. All I know is she was always good to me. I know she loved me during a time in my life when almost no one else did. So how could I not love her?

But even though I appreciate who she has been in my life I don't talk to her anymore because I don't roll like her. I haven't rolled like that in a very long time.

I hope there are no hard feelings. Every time I see her I am going to give her a hug and chit chat for a bit. But I have out grown my teen mistakes. I do not do what I used to. What I thought was fun then is different from what I think is fun now.

That's just me. That may not be the case for her or anybody else. It's not my job to pass any judgment or talk down about someone who lives a different lifestyle than me.

But the fact is I outgrew the frivolous things that I thought were fun to do when I was a teenager. Apparently not everyone does.

People change

I always try to stress the fact that we all change. Some of us change for the better, others change for the worse. Staying the same is changing for the worse, because there is no such thing as staying the same. In life we are constantly moving forwards or backwards.

There is no such thing as staying the same.

There will be people in your life that you will outgrow. There may be people who outgrow you. This doesn't mean that in either case there is any love lost. You can still love someone or be cordial without continuing to congregate with them. Learn to love people from a distance.

Change is GOOD

With time you are going to change. If you are growing you are going to take on new interests, new goals, and enjoy new pastimes. As your interests, goals, and the way you spend your leisure time changes you will naturally gravitate away from old friends and stop enjoying the things you used to do together. That's normal. The only people who don't understand that are the people who are not changing.

If your old friend is still enjoying the same things, don't feel bad that you are not. As God grows you mentally it's natural for your likes to change. Things you used to enjoy won't feel fun anymore. That's totally normal. That's a part of growing up.

People who aren't changing aren't growing. People who aren't growing can have a tendency to make you feel bad because you are. They automatically label it as you thinking you're better than them or selling out. People love to label what they don't understand.

Even more so people love to automatically assume everything they don't understand is negative. Listen; there is little you can really do to help people understand what they don't get on their own. It's really wasted energy to even try. You have to make peace with the idea that ignorance is indeed bliss.

Ignorance is indeed bliss.

Take care of you

It is important that you learn to separate yourself from people you outgrow. Even though they may not have any ill will towards you they can still pose a great threat in your life. This threat can be completely unintentional. However, it is still a threat indeed.

When you continue to circulate around friends who live a lifestyle you no longer partake in, you run a great risk of falling back in – unintentionally, of course. Even if you aren't participating fully you take a gamble on getting caught up in a situation you don't want to be involved in.

And not every case of outgrowing friends is this risky. Sometimes you simply find that you do not share the same interests anymore. When this is the case we tend to feel a slight bit of guilt. But you shouldn't. You should not feel guilty when you grow past someone else. We all grow at our own rate. Just because someone hasn't gotten where you are doesn't mean they won't get there later.

You should not feel guilty when you grow past someone else.

No matter what the case is, you are responsible for you. When dealing with friends make the decision that is best for you every time. You can't feel guilty for doing what is best for your own life. There is no value in continuing a friendship with someone who is not living on your level. You will never be much more than the people you spend your time with. So if you spend your time with people you outgrew you are destined to start to regress.

You win some, you lose some
Cutting ties with people because they are no longer on your level shouldn't be dramatic. Make a good effort to avoid offending people. Don't point out that you are cutting them off because they aren't on your level. Never make someone feel like they are beneath you. The truth is they are not. They may be living on a different level, but we are all equal. We all survive on this free air God provides. The free air you get isn't more valuable than the free air they receive.

Never make someone feel like they are beneath you.

Make sure you are not belittling people. The same people who you grew past in the last stage could have a growth spurt and pass you up by a few stages in the future. In the meantime it is important to distance yourself. But do it with love.

When you run into them out in the world it's ok to chat and get caught up. However, if you notice that they are not living like you are keep it brief. Do not get connected with them on a serious level.

Find a way to keep yourself separate that is not obvious. Make a case for just wanting to focus on you. Do not make it about them. People take offense at you pointing out their shortcomings. Strive not to be offensive.

Unfortunately, you can't always avoid offending someone no matter how hard you try. Be prepared for that. There may be some initial backlash. You can tiptoe around the subject as quietly as you want but there are some cases when the other person cannot help but notice and feel bad, hurt, or offended. That's life.

All that you can do in these cases is address it head on. Be honest and tell her you are trying to head in a different direction in life. She may become upset, but what can you do? The alternative is to continue your friendship and harbor your own growth.

No one said it'd be easy

Life is full of moments when we have to do what's right - and what's right isn't easy to do. Do it anyway. You will grow through everything you go through. If you are going to live your best life you have to do it surrounded by the best people. If your life is full of the wrong people there will be no room for the right people to come along. And if your friends are mediocre, your life will be mediocre too!

If you are going to live your best life you have to do it surrounded by the best people.

CHAPTER 10

BACKSTABBERS - WHAT HAPPENS WHEN YOU'RE NOT LOOKING

They smile in your face!

My story

I recently met a friend; let's call her Friend #1. She seemed cool from a distance. She was smart and successful. She was dependable and responsible. She was fun and like me and she kept her circle small. We grew close quickly. Before I knew it we talked every day, most days we talked numerous times. We lived real close to one another, so we started doing everything together. I brought her around my family and she brought me around hers. Things were going well. There were no warning signs.

Eventually, I introduced her to another friend of mine; let's call her Friend #2. All three of us hung and had fun together one night. Not long after our initial fun as a party of three, Friend #2 called me and asked if I was going to an event with Friend #1. It was the first I had heard about it (which was strange because Friend #1 and I did everything together). I called Friend #1 to inquire more, but she brushed it off like it wasn't something she was certain she was even attending, like she was just talking about it with Friend #2.

I let it go, not thinking much of it, until it happened again just days later. I was talking to Friend #2 when she said she had just got off the phone with Friend #1 and she had asked her to a movie. I found that peculiar since I had just gotten off the phone with Friend #1 prior to calling Friend #2. There was no mention to me about seeing a movie. But thinking nothing of it I brushed it off, too.

A few weeks later, Friend #2 sends me a text asking me if I was attending a party that Friend #1 was having. Again, this was news to me. I simply replied, "No". Not long after, Friend #1 called and invited me to her party. I passed since I already had plans, but I knew something was suspicious about the invitation.

As time went on I began to observe the situation a little more closely. Friend #2 called and invited me out and I went. While we were out we took pictures and posted them on online. Apparently Friend #1 had seen the photos and didn't appreciate not being invited, because she sent me a long dramatic text saying she was really hurt that we went out without inviting her. That threw me for a loop.

I remember I was driving and I pulled over to respond. Her text was just what I needed to verify that I wasn't paranoid before. I explained to her that Friend #2 and I were friends doing things before she and I had even met, therefore there was no need for her to feel "hurt" if we choose to go out without her in the future. Of course she tried to cover it up and say she was just joking, but there's a little truth behind every joke. I could tell by the way she had phrased her message that there was nothing funny about it.

So with that being straight I moved on. Friend #2 and I were going out of town on a road trip. I extended an invite to Friend #1, but she couldn't make it. While on the trip I got a chance to tell Friend #2 about the text incident a few weeks prior. She found it shocking that Friend #1 would even take that stance, considering that Friend #1 had made numerous invitations for the two of them to go out without me! She began to tell me about numerous occasions when Friend #1 was trying to go hang out with her, without me.

Here it was I had introduced the two of them to one another. Yet Friend #1 treated me like I had no right to hang out with my friend, Friend #2, without her, and all along she, Friend #1, had gone behind my back and invited Friend #2 to several, not just two or three but numerous, events and outings without me? Where do they do that?

I never called Friend #1 again after I returned! I wasn't jealous. They are both grown women and have a right to hang out with one another with or without me. That doesn't bother me at all. I didn't catch feelings about that fact that they would have hung out without me (though Friend #2 opted to pass on every invite, so they never actually did hang out).

It's the shady sneakiness that Friend #1 displayed that I despise. It wasn't major what Friend #1 did. Not major at all. However, it was a surefire sign that I couldn't fully trust her. If I know anything I know that there are always small signs that come before bigger signs. I'm getting better with age at catching the signs earlier. If I hadn't cut off Friend #1 early, then she would have certainly done something else, probably something that actually matters.

Guilty people always think you're doing the same thing

The problem for me lies in the implications, not the act. You see, Friend #1 revealed her true colors with her text message. That was the sign. Had she never taken offense to me and Friend #2 going out without her I may not have even noticed her sneaky ways later.

Oftentimes guilty people become paranoid that you are doing to them what they are doing to you! I've seen it happen in a plethora of different scenarios. I have seen cheating boyfriends (and girlfriends) accuse their mate of cheating…because they become paranoid that someone is getting away with what they are getting away with!

Let's say Friend #1 never sent that text message. Let's say Friend #2 had accepted one of Friend #1's offers to hang out - just the two of them. I probably would have thought nothing of it. What would it matter to me if they did something together? That would pose no threat to me.

All of my friends have other friends that I do not necessarily know. I do not feel obligated to attend every outing my friends attend. That's absurd.

I will admit that it can be a bit awkward if two friends you introduce quickly cut you out and become chummy. But that is not always the case either because there are times when two people just gel instantly. That isn't always a threat to the middle-man/woman. And that isn't an implication that they do not like the middle-woman, either. Only insecure people feel threatened by things like that.

But that is not the situation here. When Friend #1 sent me a message about how hurt she was that we did not invite her it implied that she felt threatened - not just left out. We hadn't all met each other together. She hadn't introduced me to Friend #2. She knew I knew Friend #2 before I knew her, so why was she threatened by the fact that I was hanging out with my friend?

There can only be two explanations for her concern. Either she was worried that Friend #2 would reveal to me her own sneaky invites if we were alone, or she was worried that I was doing what she was obviously doing: trying to have Friend #2 to myself. I know how crazy it sounds, but like I said before who knows what goes on in the mind of a hater? Whatever it is, it's not logical.

When I met Friend #1 I made the mistake of assuming she was like me because she had an incredibly small circle of friends. Now, looking back, I see it was probably because she was stabbing people in the back!

The calm before the storm

By no means is what happened in this case some severe act of back-stabbery. Not at all! But it certainly was a sign that my so-called friend was sneaky. Sneaky people stab you in the back. I am too old to take gambles on people. I do not go behind my friends' backs and do things that could remotely be considered sneaky. I have a zero tolerance clause for any shadiness. And you should too.

Be very observant of things that just don't feel right to you. Woman's intuition is a very real thing. That funny feeling you get is not paranoia, it is intuition. Learn to trust your body when it gives you signs that something feels off. Sure, my story with Friend #1 is not traumatic or even dramatic…but it would have been!

Pay attention to the small, minor, and seemingly unimportant signs people give you about who they are. Friend #1 wouldn't have become a better friend with time. She wasn't going to change her ways and feel guilty about what she'd done. She probably still doesn't see any fault in what happened. There is a great possibility that she has no idea why I even cut her off. But I did. I never rang her phone again. Why, because I trusted that little funny feeling I had. Who knows what I avoided? We'll never know exactly what would have happened, but I know something would have.

Pay attention to small, minor, and seemingly unimportant signs that people give you about who they are.

I didn't even broadcast my feeling to Friend #2. That would have been a hater move. I didn't feel compelled to imply to Friend #2 that she shouldn't be friends with Friend #1. That's not my job. Friend #2 would have to find out about Friend #1 on her own. I never even asked her if she talked to Friend #1. That's not my business. As long as Friend #1 was out of my life, I was good. (I have to assume since Friend #2 never talked about Friend #1 that they didn't talk, but again I don't know that for sure).

They smile in your face...

A backstabber is someone you think you can trust until you find out after the fact that they betrayed you, acted against you, or went after something that was yours. All backstabbers want something. I don't know for sure what Friend #1 wanted, but I'd guess she wanted the friendship that I shared with Friend #2 (yes, I know how petty that sounds, but Frienemies are often very petty).

Pay attention to the warning signs. In every situation there will most certainly be a sign. Strive to heed the signs and take action immediately. Once you trust yourself enough to know the signs and cut people off you will rid yourself of horror stories. You do not need an excuse to cut a friend off.

We so often make the mistake of feeling obligated to obtain hard-core evidence on a person before we act. You do not owe an explanation to people when you cut them off! You can simply break ties with a person based on the fact that you can. Say you did it because you wanted to. As a matter of fact, don't feel responsible for saying anything at all. You owe no explanations. Feel empowered not to answer any questions.

Once you get used to doing this it gets easier and easier every time. I'm good for just disappearing into the sunset on a foe. All it takes is a good gut feeling and I'm out! Remember, you are better safe than sorry. These people are getting more and more cruel - take no chances!

You are better safe than sorry.

It's too late to apologize

If you overlook the signs until after it's too late, then forgive her and forget her quickly. When people go behind your back and betray you that is not something you can ever let slide! It's one strike and she is out. Do not play around with this logic. The first time it's shame on her, but every time after that it's shame on you!

I know a person is a fool when they can tell me more than one story about the same person doing something bad to them. If the same person does two bad things to you then you are an idiot. Do not allow someone to play you for a fool. I have no sympathy for people who continue to let the same person victimize them. If you are dumb enough to let them stay in your life, why should I empathize with you? Do not be weak. Find a way to put some permanent space between you and that person. There is always away. Protect yourself at all costs.

Do not allow someone to play you for a fool.

Backstabbers are heartless. They aren't going to suddenly feel guilty and remorseful for what they did. You are responsible for you. If you do not protect yourself no one else can.

CHAPTER 11

FIGHTING IN THE FRIEND-ZONE - FLAG ON THE PLAY

Violations

Pick your battles…

Even the best of friends have disagreements. No two people agree on everything all the time. It's a given that friends will disagree. But there are healthy and unhealthy ways to address your differences.

How your friend handles herself in a disagreement is a dead giveaway as to if she is a Friend or FRIENEMY! Pay attention.

What you are disagreeing over really matters when it comes to how she reacts. When you really love someone you care about how you debate with them. A great sign that someone loves you is when they concede even if they don't agree with you. That isn't to say you shouldn't concede to her at times, as well. But if you find your friend is escalating the argument, and then realize she is not a friend at all!

Only a Frienemy is careless enough with your relationship to escalate the situation. When you really care about someone and value who they are to you, you are careful to avoid crossing the line. When a person is willing to escalate the situation by taking it from bad to worse they are willing to risk losing you altogether. Real friends don't want to lose you as a friend. Real friends are always willing to agree to disagree. Fake friends couldn't care less about your feelings. This is true in every scenario.

Real friends are always willing to agree to disagree.

The verbal assault

Argument etiquette is rarely taught, but we could all benefit from learning it. There is a healthy way to disagree with someone, especially someone who is a friend.

At no point when communicating with your friend should you be disrespected. This is true no matter what the subject is or how extreme the level of disagreement. Two grown women should be able to get their points across with no yelling and zero name calling!

Once your conversation reaches the point that you are intentionally insulted, consider that a verbal assault. At that point the conversation is over! In all situations you demand your respect! There is never an exception to this.

You must be strong enough to recognize that someone who verbally assaults you does not respect you. There is no such thing as a friendship where one friend doesn't respect the other. The moment you are disrespected the friendship is over - forever.

Sure, things are said in the heat of the moment and the height of passion. But you should know that those are the moments where deep truths are revealed. People do not have time to think of something insulting that they never thought about before. It may be the first time that you heard it from that person's mouth, but it was not the first time they thought it! When someone tells you what they really think of you believe them!

Sure, a good spirited person will eventually apologize for what they said against you. But do not make the mistake of believing that a sincere apology is rectification enough to forgive and move on. An apology is enough to forgive and forget. Accept the apology; express that all is forgiven and then explain that the friendship is permanently null and void! It's over.

An apology usually means "I'm sorry that I hurt you". It doesn't mean "I do not really think what I said was true". Learn the difference. Oftentimes people are genuinely sorry that they hurt you. That is different from not meaning what they said. Many apologies end with "I didn't mean it". Ten times out of ten that is a lie. Of course they mean it, that's their real thought about you, however they didn't mean for you to know about it! Either way, recognize that the friendships over.

The physical assault

It is pathetic to think that two adults, women at that, who considered one another friends would ever get to the point where things are going to get physical. But sadly it happens.

Growing up, my mother taught me when someone put their hands on me to hit them back. Today, I teach my kids that same philosophy. Not because I want to promote violence, but because I believe in promoting self-respect.

I want my children to know that it is not optional for others to respect them. I want their position to always be "you are going to respect me at all times, rather you like me or not." Therefore, I tell them in very certain terms if someone hits you hit them back ten times harder!

But they are kids. Grown-ups should be able to dislike someone without the need to ever put their hands on one another. That's a part of maturity. That's a part of class. That's a part of self-control. We all come across people we do not like, people who bring out the worst in us, and people who push our buttons, but there is really no excuse to get physical.

Grown-ups should be able to dislike someone without the need to ever put their hands on one another.

If you have a friend who assaults you, there should be zero doubt that she is a FRIENEMY! I do not care what you did to upset her; she should never cross the line from arguing to fighting. If there is ever an instance that you are physically assaulted, do not hesitate to call the police! Your motto must be "hit me and you will go to jail"! You should be pressing charges and filing for a restraining order!

You can't play around with people who get violent. In today's times too many people end up dead and in jail behind petty disagreements. With your luck you'll fight back and end up dead, or end up in jail. Scratch that, call 911 and turn her ass in A.S.A.P!

The prisons are full of women who are locked up behind incidents that went wrong with a so-called friend! The cemeteries are full the bodies of women who were killed by a so-called friend. Don't underestimate how far things can go. No one ever plans to go from a fist-fight to death row, but it has happened thousands upon thousands of times!

Keep your hands to yourself. The knife cuts both ways. You should be implementing the same respect that your expect. You should be giving your friends the same considerations that they owe you.

You will not always agree with every word that comes out of your friend's mouth. Your friends do not have to see every point of view you have in every situation. Expect that everyone is different and that there are going to be times when you and your friends disagree. That is fine. The world would be a boring place if everyone thought like you, liked what you liked and agreed with everything you said.

Even good friends in great friendships see the same things differently. So what? As long as you are not verbally or physically assaulted you should assume that a minor disagreement is natural.

Take the liberty of being the friend who is the first to concede. Ask yourself; is this subject worth losing this friend? If not, find a way to change the subject and move past the conversation. Be the one who de-escalates an argument. The bigger person is the one who sees the big picture.

CHAPTER 12

YOUR FRIENDS & YOUR MAN - WHAT'S THE LIMIT?

He said…She said

The chicken or the egg

Our romantic relationships and our platonic relationships should never cause conflict with one another. Yet they so often do. And when they do you are generally caught in the middle. Most women in this situation feel more loyalty to the person that came first into their lives, whether it is the friend or the spouse.

Assuming your relationship is good your loyalty should always be to your spouse! This is most certainly the case if you are married. A marriage is a union between two people who agree to consider the other person like they consider themselves. It's an act of two becoming one. So you cannot rightfully side with your friend over your husband.

(Now, if your relationship is not good you should not even be reading this yet. You should be reading Volume 1 in this series about men)

Your loyalty should always be to your spouse.

In the case of a disagreement between your friend and your spouse, in which you honestly believe your friend is correct and your spouse is incorrect, then you have an obligation to help your spouse see things the right way.

However, oftentimes the friend came before the man. In cases where a friend has been a part of your life longer than your man you naturally tend to feel a great sense of loyalty to her. After all, she has likely become like a sister to you. I can appreciate the strain it puts on you to side against her, especially in cases where she has already proven herself to be your true friend.

It's always an uncomfortable situation when your friends and your man clash. But your alliance should be to your man. A real friend will not only understand that but she will respect it.

How close is too close

Sometimes the problem isn't that they don't get along. Sometime the problem is that they get along too much. Let's just be honest, it doesn't matter who the woman is, there is an uneasiness when it comes to any woman being too close to your man!

Not all women are sneaky and trying to sleep with your man. However, you should assume they are. If a woman, any woman, is being too flirty, chatty, or just too close to your man you should assume the worst. Though the worst is not always the case, it's almost impossible to know when it is and when it isn't.

This is why, to avoid the headache, stress, and guess-work, you need to be the one who sets real boundaries. Don't have your friend constantly around your man. When you are hanging out with her it should be girls' night, not date night plus one. On occasions when you and your man are doing something and she is invited she needs to be accompanied by some sort of date of her own. Three really is a crowd. The three of you do not need to go places together. If she doesn't have someone who can join then she can't join either.

Three really is a crowd.

The only time I'd even consider making an exception is when she is married or attached and for some reason her significant other cannot attend, but he has given his blessing for her to go. And this only applies when her man and your man are both well acquainted and get along fine. I only make this exception due to the low rate of issues when two men respect each other. Under that circumstance it is rare that either your man or your friend would take a chance at making a pass at the other person, out of fear they'd be rejected and then exposed.

I know you know your friend. I know you know that she isn't like that. I know you know that your man isn't attracted to her anyway. I know that you know a lot…but I also know that there have been tens of thousands of cases where all of the above have been known by a woman who was still betrayed by her man and her friend hooking up.

Many times what you think you know turns out to be worthless. Shit happens. These types of betrayals happen all the time!

It happened to my sister. Her good friend, who was also her son's aunt, had moved to town. Being nice, my sister brought her to a party that my sister's current boyfriend was hosting. She thought it'd be a great opportunity for her to meet people. Months later she found out that they'd exchanged numbers at the party. They had been having an affair for months! Everyone was shocked! They were the only two people who knew. None of us had a clue. There were no signs, but it was going on behind her back. She was devastated. She was hurt. And, to make it better, the only reason they told her was because they had decided they were going to be together.

Do not assume the impossible will not take place. Learn to expect what you least expect. People you never expect will let you down. Don't be naïve. Any two consenting adults can have a weak moment of bad judgment. Do your part to help them avoid such.

Learn to expect the things you least expect.

A happy medium

It is your own responsibility to locate a happy medium between your relationship and your friendships. Every woman has a different need when it comes to how much time they spend with their friends vs. how much time they spend with their man. This need can vary depending their current relationship and their current friends.

You could be dating someone who works a lot or travels often, so you have more time to spend socializing with the girls. Or you could be madly head over heels with a man you can't stand to separate from and find that you have little to no time available for your friends. In either case there is nothing wrong with that. You need to figure out what you need to feel balanced and format your life around that.

When you calculate how you would like to spend your time, be honest with yourself about what you want. If you try to please someone else and not yourself you are only causing yourself problems for the future.

If you are with a man who seems way too needy and, out of guilt, you spend less time than you want with your friends, you will become resentful towards him. On the flip side, if your friends are harping on you because you are always "boo'ed up" now and you allow that to force you to hang with them when you'd rather be with him, you'll begin to resent them.

Be honest with yourself about what type of balance works for you. Then be clear with your man and your friends about how you want things to be for you. There is no fault in whatever balance you need to be happy. Do not feel guilty either way. The fault lies when you are not being clear and upfront about what you want and need. Just be honest with people. Either they can get with it or get behind it.

CHAPTER 13

FRIENDS AND MONEY - A BAD MIX

Oil & Water

A dangerous combination

Nothing breaks up a friendship faster than money issues. It has been long been said that people should not do business with family or friends. It's a recipe for disaster, no doubt. However, what about loans?

I've said before that I think good friends are willing to use their resources in order to help a friend who is truly in need. Certainly money would be included in those resources. However, I am strongly against loaning money to friends.

When I was younger and living paycheck to paycheck I borrowed money from all of my friends at one point or another. Sometimes I borrowed a little, sometimes I borrowed a lot. However, there wasn't a friend or family member within arm's reach who I didn't hit up for a loan. And I paid it back every time on time. My problem then wasn't that I was not fiscally responsible, the problem was that I didn't make enough money to make ends meet. But, whatever the case may be for your friend, I strongly advise you to never loan them any money.

I can admit I am blessed. Now I am the lender and do not have to borrow. I get bombarded by people who have this financial emergency and that financial emergency. It's nonstop. And everyone thinks because I have it they should get it. That's when I started to recognize most people do not deserve a loan.

Most people who constantly need to borrow money are not being responsible with the money that they have. They do not bother to save. They go to the mall with their spare change and then one week later a bill pops up that they have to pay right away. That's called being irresponsible. Don't feel obligated to help irresponsible people out of a jam. Let their lights get cut off instead of paying the bill and see if they do not learn a lesson.

Most people who constantly need to borrow money are not being responsible with the money they have.

The problem with helping friends who are not financially responsible is that they never learn how to become financially responsible. These people are always full of worthless excuses! None of these excuses ever point to the fact that it is their own fault. They are always a victim of unfortunate and untimely circumstances. Don't take the bait.

Simply explain that you are not going to be able to do it. You are not responsible for your friend's irresponsible decisions. If you really love someone you will allow them to learn how to avoid being in the same situation in the future.

When I was borrowing money, people always loaned it to me if they had it because they knew I would pay them back. However, as much as I appreciated what they did, I realized that it didn't help me become more responsible. It didn't help me realize that I was always living above my means.

It's important to help our friends; especially when we have it to give. However, you are not really helping a person if they are just going to end up in the same situation again later.

When friends get into financial trouble because of their own fiscal irresponsibility, don't get involved. Do not be an enabler. Let your adult friend figure out her financial problem without you coming to her rescue. That's how you help someone. Like the saying goes, give a man a fish and he'll eat for a day, but teach a man to fish and he can eat for a lifetime. Stop just giving your friend fish and start trying to teach her some fiscal responsibility for the long haul.

So I stress to you, never give a friend a loan. The moment that there is an issue with her paying you back the whole relationship will be in turmoil. Remember, this person wasn't responsible with her own money, what makes you think she will care more about yours?

Be nice, but opt out. It's not your place to be in your friend's finances.

Never give a friend a loan.

Pre-qualified
Not every friend has issues with spending their money wisely. Some are very financially mature; however circumstances have arisen that cause them to need a loan.

That happens to us all. Maybe she has saved, but something big and unexpected happened that caused her to need more than she has. It happens. However, in this case I advise not loaning her the money!

Never loan your friends money. Never loan your family money. When you loan your money it's like entering into a business contract with someone. Though, unlike business contracts, personal loans between friends are usually not written down. This can cause big headaches when there is a discrepancy about the payback agreement.

Never loan your friends money.

Trust me; it's very uncomfortable seeing someone who owes you money out spending money on anything. It doesn't matter if they aren't even due to pay you back yet. You can't help but be bothered to see that they are at the mall, at the bar, at the car wash…or doing anything that costs anything. It's annoying having to watch them spend money leisurely when they owe you. So my policy is never loan your friends under any circumstance.

The moment you loan a friend money and they can't pay you back as agreed, there goes the relationship. You do not want to lose a good friendship behind a loan. But it happens.

If you got it flaunt it!

Now that we have clearly established that it's never ok to loan money to a friend, let's cover what you should do to help a friend in need. If your friend has a financial problem and you have the money to give, give it to her! I repeat: if you have the money to *GIVE*…give it to her.

Give it and don't look back. Don't ask for it back. Just give it to her. See, if you can afford to give it without needing it back then you can afford to help her. If you have it but cannot afford to give it away, then you can't afford to risk losing it in a loan and you shouldn't be willing to risk losing your friend if she can't repay you.

When people ask me for money or loans I say no unless I can afford to give it without getting it back. Granted, when they call and ask they know I have that amount. But if I cannot afford to part with that amount at that time, I say no. I don't make them sign promissory notes so that I know I can get it back. I don't stress to them the importance of repayment because I can't afford to not have it. I just say no. Flat out I can't right now.

But if they catch me during a good time financially, or if they only need a small amount, I give it gladly. I give it quickly. I go out of my way to bring to them. Because I'm happy to help and I know that I am where I am because people helped me. So I feel blessed to be a blessing and strive to show it.

But even then I make it very clear that I am giving them the money to have, not loaning it to them. Not giving it to them because I know God is going to bless me for it (I crack up when I hear people say that foolishness). I'm just giving it because I want to give to the people I care about.

Sometimes they feel compelled to repay even though I'm not requiring them to. I try to avoid that. I really try to not have them pay me back even if they want to. I try to offset the loan through a service or something else because I do not want to be viewed as a banker.

When lightning strikes twice

On rare occasions lightning strikes twice. It is because of this that I do my very best to avoid accepting repayment for any money that I give out. If my friend finds herself in the same predicament later I want to avoid her coming to me next time. But when people know you have it, know you did it for them before and know that they paid you back in full and on time, they start to view you like their own personal banker!

With some people it never stops; especially people who live above their means. It's always something. Something pops up that they need help paying immediately. When they establish a borrowing system with you they begin make a habit of coming to you because they know you have it and they feel you know they will repay it.

Nope take a pass on that.

Remember, only help when you can afford to give it away and never think about it again. Try not to accept it back because people tend to believe that makes you a bank and they have a great re-payment history with you. Just stop while you're ahead. Just because you have it doesn't obligate you to give it. You want to be teaching people to fish, not fishing for them.

Just because you have it doesn't obligate you to give it.

CHAPTER 14

NEW FRIENDS VS. OLD FRIENDS - THE COMPETITION

The battle between good and evil

Old school, New School

As we grow and our interests change we meet new people along the way. Our new friends tend to reflect our current self. They share our mutual interests and represent who were are striving to become. But before they came along we had old friends. These are the friends we grew up with. The friends who helped mold us into who we are today and the friends who represent who we were in our past.

Unfortunately, these two groups of friends can tend to be extremely different. Their differences can keep them from blending well. Generally speaking, you don't usually have to account for the two friend types spending much time with one another. But on rare occasions, like your birthday or wedding, you may have the gang all in. And it can definitely be stressful!

It's not always true, but usually it's the old friend who takes offense at the new friend. It's hard to see someone move in on your longtime friend and connect with her in ways you used to. And when your old friend starts feeling this way it's you who usually heeds the guilt.

Understand that such is life. As friends we really shouldn't experience jealousy when our friends get new friends. Old friends tend to feel left behind when we become close to someone new. That can't always be avoided.

It is important that you do not stunt your own personal growth out of the guilt of leaving someone else behind. It is necessary that you grow and your interests mature. It is equally important that you meet new people who share your current desires and interests. This is what life is all about.

No two people are going to grow at the exact same rate. Granted, the older you become the less you grow, but that means the younger you are the more rapid your growth will be. So how can you have a friend from High School or College and, fifteen or twenty years later, you are both still on the exact same level? It's not realistic. The only time that this is the case is when you are not growing.

Just because you have become close to a new friend and began to drift away from an old friend is not reason to end your old friendship. Try to find time for your old friend when the two of you can do something that you both still enjoy.

Friendships are not marriages - so don't view them as lifetime commitments.

But if your old friend (or new friend) is set on being a problem or causing you stress, let them go. Friendships are not marriages. There is no "Til death do us part" clause involved. When friendships stop being fun they should stop being friendships.

When friendships stop being fun they should stop being friendships.

Go forward in life feeling no guilt for who you have to leave behind. Not everyone will make it to your next season. If old friends have proven themselves as good friends, try to maintain the friendship. Sometimes, as life's journey moves us around, we lose connections and contact with friends we once had and begin new connections.

However, if your old friends are jealous of your new friendships, kick them to the curb. Your friends have no right to make you feel any type of way about who you choose to become close with. There should be no guilt associated with who you have befriended.

The same is true for new friends. They shouldn't catch feelings about your relationship with your old friends. There is no justification for that.

Friends are just friends. Never let them dictate who you spend your time with. You owe your friends nothing more than to be a good friend to them. If they don't like another friend of yours, they don't have to be friends with her. And they don't have to be friends with you either. They can move around and make space for another new friend to come along!

CHAPTER 15

HOW TO BREAK-UP WITH A FRIENEMY - GOODBYES

Tips for cutting ties and staying drama free in the process

So you have found a Frienemy

So you have determined that your friend is actually a Frienemy. Now what? Let me be clear. You must cut them off, right now. You cannot put off separating yourself from a Frienemy. The only person in danger is you. The longer you continue the friendship the more you submit yourself to the consequences of your Frienemy's action.

At the first sign of trouble, you need to take action and cease the friendship once and for all. The longer you allow a Frienemy to stay in your life the more horror stories you will have to tell later. Leopards don't change their spots. Frienemies do not magically see the error of their ways and transform back into real friends.

The longer you allow a Frienemy to stay in your life the more horror stories you will have to tell later.

Do not bother having an intervention. Bringing a Frienemy's actions to their attention doesn't work. Either they become defensive, lie about it, or they realize you are on to them and perfect their evil ways to be less noticeable.

Once you recognize a Frienemy's identity you have no choice but to end the relationship. Immediately! Don't live in fear. Don't be weak. If you have known this person for a long time, it could be incredibly hard to picture your life without them. Do it anyway. Choose you. Choose to ensure that everyone you consider a friend is an actual friend. If you don't do it, you will certainly regret it later.

You must learn to expect what you tolerate from others. Don't lie to yourself and say that you recognize the Frienemy in a person and therefore you will only deal with them on certain levels. That does not work. You cannot dabble here and there with a toxic friend. There is no such thing as half-friends or party friends. I have tried it all. It does not work. You need a whole friend. That is the only kind of friend there is: a whole friend. You need a friend who you can trust in every area of your whole life, not just a section here and a section there.

Do not bother trying to keep them as associates, either. You don't need to associate with Frienemies. What good is it to have someone you occasionally associate with that you already know is a bad friend? Be smart. What good can a Frienemy really help you produce in your life?

There is no excuse for continuing to associate with a Frienemy. None. Never.

There is no excuse for continuing to associate with a Frienemy.

Learn to slice without being cut

Try to cut off your Frienemy without causing excess or unnecessary drama. It isn't always possible, but you should definitely try. What you don't need to do is go out with a bang. Do not be vengeful. Whatever your Frienemy has done, be ok with letting them get away with it. Vengeance is mine, said the Lord. He didn't say Vengeance is mine unless you want to make it yours, or you see an easy way to get them back.

It is not your job to make sure people learn their lesson. Be ok with the idea that your Frienemy may never know how her actions hurt or affected you. We must accept the things we do not understand. You may not understand how or why someone could do something the way they did. That's ok.

Learn to forgive people for things they do to you. It doesn't matter in the long run. They cannot stop your shine. Your life is going to be better without them. If you absolutely must get them back, then get them back by letting them see how great your life is after them. But even that is not important. What is important is that you move on - Frienemy free!

Try not to make it immediately obvious that you have cut her off. Let your Frienemy figure it out gradually. When she calls, do not feel obligated to answer every time. When you do answer, just let her do the talking. Barely respond, don't ask questions and act like you are just listening. Don't keep the conversation moving. Once she is done talking, tell her you gotta go.

Don't answer her questions. Don't engage in her conversation. If she called to tell you something, listen silently and, when she finishes, get off the phone.

It's even better if you don't answer. It may be strange if you don't answer any of their calls at first. If you previously talked on the phone or texted all the time it may be alarming if you just suddenly stop altogether withdraw yourself from the situation naturally. Be a judge of when it is appropriate for you not to answer or reply, and don't. If you know she is calling and does not want anything, let it ring. If she sends you a text that is not a question, do not reply.

You do not need to be sitting on the phone shooting the breeze with these fools. If she texts you a question, reply with simple one word answers, or don't reply at all.

It is important that you are not mad or rude. Be cool. Be nonchalant. Be easy. Be relaxed. You do not need to imply in any way that you are separating yourself from her. She will figure it out eventually on her own. If she asks if you are mad at her, simply say no. That's it. If she asks what is wrong, say nothing. Because that is the truth?? nothing is wrong with you. Everything is right. You are removing a negative person from your life. What's not right about that?

Don't act funny. Just be yourself. Try to avoid making it too obvious that you're cutting ties with this person. It's not about what the other person knows or learns it is only about what you know and learn. You are not here to teach a Frienemy anything. You are here to live your best life now.

You are here to live your best life now!

Be Anti-Social networking

Facebook and other social networks keep us connected to people we should be disconnected from. Usually deleting or un-friend-ing a person is too obvious. My suggestion is for you to go in and "hide" her from your news feed first. This way you won't see anything she posts. While you are in the early stages of cutting off a close friend-turned-Frienemy reduce your postings and status updates drastically, especially if the person was previously active on your posts.

Social networks keep us connected to people we should be disconnected from.

You do not need to open a line of communication up about anything. You don't want to update your status to "It's raining by my house" and have her turn around and comment on it with a question like, "How hard is it raining?" Now you either have to reply, which is just opening up a line of communication you don't need, or ignore her, which just makes it obvious that you're cutting her off. No matter how simple or unrelated your posts may be, it gives the other person the opportunity to communicate with you. Keep your posts to a minimum for a while.

This too shall pass and you can get back to your normal posting pace later. Have the patience to let things gradually fade away. There is no rushing the process when you do it right. In order to cut ties with the least amount of drama, do it slowly. You don't have a friend for years and then cut the friendship off in two weeks. It's a progression. Let it fade away over time. She'll get the message.

Once time has passed and the air is clear, then go in and unfriend her. Give it a month or more. Once things have died down and all communication has stopped that is when it's best to go in and make permanent changes. If you have done everything correctly, she won't immediately notice that you have un-friended her.

What you absolutely should not do is post anything even slightly related to what happened or how you feel about it. I am so sick of seeing these long Facebook statuses of how Person A is cutting ties with Person B because Person B is a bad person, blah, blah, blah. That is tacky. Let the haters do the hating. Operate with class. Never let them know what you are thinking.

Never let them know what you are thinking.

The wrong thing to do is to scream to the world what happened, how you feel about what happened, and what you are doing about what happened. The right thing to do is to do whatever it is you need to do and do it under the radar. Do not always feel compelled to talk about your feelings with others on a platform for the world to see. If you really want someone to talk to about it, the best person is someone completely unassociated with the Frienemy, not your Facebook timeline.

Be comfortable letting things roll off your back. Do not respond when she posts something or says something that gets under your skin. You should be motivated by insuring she never knows how you feel about it. No matter how hard she hits or how low she goes you never reply. She doesn't mean enough to you to reply - that's what the message you're sending should be.

Let them learn the hard way!
Oftentimes you and she may have mutual friends. Your etiquette is seriously important here. If someone is a bad friend to you, chances are high that she will be a bad friend to others. However, you should not feel obligated to warn your friends. You should also not spend your time bad mouthing her to others. Let them observe the situation from where they are.

A smart person will recognize that what she did to you she will do to them, too. And if she doesn't, who wants a friend that did that to someone else anyway? Let people make their own decisions on if and how to deal with your Frienemies.

Be a class act. Take the high road. When you are associating with a mutual friend, do not take the opportunity to explain what happened to you. If they ask why you are not friends anymore be extremely general with your reply. Do not go into detail and explain your feelings. Give an honest but vague answer. Something like, "I just noticed some things that made me feel uncertain." Answers like that give the respect of an answer without really saying anything at all. If they ask you to elaborate say something like, "I really don't want to get into it." Then change the subject to something light, positive, and unrelated.

Be an Army of 1
Resist the urge to get mutual friends on your team. That is not appropriate. Do not try to build an alliance of people to go against your ex-friend. Be confident in who you are. Only a weak person would feel insecure about sharing a mature friend that's an ex-friend-turned-Frienemy.

If you have concerns about your mutual friend's disloyalty then cut her off, too. You do not need a reason or full proof in order to stop a friendship. If your mutual friend is a good friend you will not get the sense that her continuing to be friends with your Frienemy makes her disloyal to you. Follow the feeling you get in your gut. Women's intuition is a very real thing. If you sense something is funny, you are not paranoid…something is funny.

If you have to cut ties with a mutual friend merely on suspicion, then follow the same nonchalant, quiet format that you cut your Frienemy off with. Gradual reduced communication followed by total and complete cut-off. You do not need a reason to stop being friends with anyone at any time.

You do not need a reason to stop being friends with anyone at any time.

I am notorious for pulling disappearing acts on Frienemies. The reason is I know that I do not need an excuse to disassociate myself from anyone. I can do it just because I want to with no reason given. That is my right. And that is your right. Stop digging for evidence and looking for signs in order to have a reason.

If you get that funny feeling act on it, don't wait. You do not have to explain yourself to anyone. With the exception of your own children, feel free to walk away from anyone you want for no reason. Walk away just because you want to.

This is your life!
     This is your one life. What you do with it is your choice. Take full responsibility for everything that happens to you and everything others do to you. No one is a part of your life without your permission. There are no victims with regards to friends. You choose your friends. If you choose bad friends who do bad things to you, then accept that you made that choice. If you choose to overlook the bad things that people do, then do not feel sorry for yourself when people do bad things to you.
     People only treat you how you allow them to treat you. If you opt to look beyond the obvious signs that a friend is really a Frienemy you will undoubtedly live with the consequences. You are not the exception to the rule.
     Make the wise decision not to take chances in your life. Make the choice to ensure you are removing Frienemies after their first offense. If not, the time you waste will be your own.

People only treat you the way you allow them to treat you.

It's so hard to say goodbye
     Ending a long friendship is sad. It's like ending a long time romantic relationship. We go through it emotionally, but we recover. When you accept that it has to be done, allow yourself time to mourn, and do what is necessary to reap the rewards in the end. You move into a new season. And you are blessed for being obedient! Don't miss your blessing because you are still connected to a Frienemy.

CHAPTER 16

THE FRIEND IN YOU - HOW TO BE THE BEST OF THE BEST

The Mirror Effect

You get what you give

In order to have good friends you need to be a good friend. Consistency is key here. You must possess the traits of a good friend at all times. In life you get what you give.

Don't expect that your friends should be willing to do anything more for you than you are willing to do for them. And in many cases you should be prepared to model for them what a good friend really is.

In life what you wish for others is what you will get. Therefore it is extremely important that you are wishing others well. What you give to others is what you will get in return. So give your friends your best!

Give your friends your best!

Best friends

The best friends are positive friends. They always speak a blessing over your life. They always see the glass as half-full. They get a great vision in everything you do and every situation you face.

The best friends are full of love. They make you feel supported and secure. They see you as an important part of their life. You never feel like an outsider when you're hanging with the best friends.

The best friends are eager to help you resolve problems. They are willing to be wrong when you are right. They love to celebrate and honor you. The best friends don't feel like friends at all: they feel like family.

That's what you need to be to your friends. You need to be the best friend. You need to exemplify all of these things constantly. You should be never changing and always consistent. A good friend isn't moody because every time they see or speak to you they are instantly cheered up. You should be the light that draws your friends near.

You should be the light that draws your friends near.

You should feel a sense of responsibility for the people that God has placed in your life. You should be filling them up with positivity and continuous love. Never take advantage of the relationship. Everyone comes into your life for a reason. Though you may never know the purpose, it still exists. Appreciate that your friend was given to you by God for some purpose. Do not neglect the union.

Be available when your friends call. Be eager to celebrate your friends and be rewarding. Be a people up lifter. Make it a personal challenge to make people better. Ask yourself, what can I give to my friend to help her life be better?

Keep a listening ear. The best friends are easy to talk to and always ready to listen. Keep a giving heart. What's yours is hers and what's hers is yours.

Avoid being critical or judgmental. The last thing your friend needs is to come to you and leave feeling judged. Your shoulder should be a judgment-free zone. If your friends can't come to your with their problems, who can they go to?

Give the best advice you can give. We counsel our friends. The value of a good friend is in having a pair of eyes viewing the situation from the outside looking in. They have a totally different perspective on the scenario. That's why friends value our opinions. Don't be lackluster in your advice. Take a good look from all perspectives and be the voice of reasoning that your friend needs. Being a good friend is about telling your friend what's right as opposed to just telling them what they want to hear. Don't be a yes ma'am. But be the best ma'am.

Don't be hating

Common sense tells me that we should all know that there's no room for hate in our friendships. However, if there is one thing I know for sure it's that common sense is far from common. So let me break it down for you.

Don't be jealous of your friend. Friends are going to go through their season of blessings just like everyone else will. They may get their season when we are going through a not-so-blessed season. Celebrate and be happy for her anyway. Be her biggest cheerleader. We all go through this thing called life. We all face our own battles and trials and tribulations. It's ok for someone other than you to win sometimes.

There are enough blessings in Heaven for us all to have some. Whatever God does in her life he can do something in yours that's on the same level. But take your eyes off her blessing. Her blessing isn't for you. So let her enjoy it. Help her enjoy it.

So often friends are ok with you doing well until you get more than they have- then it's a problem! Don't be that kind of friend. Recognize that when your friend wins you win, too. It is difficult enough being in competition with those who are against us - don't be in competition with the people who are for you, too.

When you get blessed you want people to be happy for you! Return the favor. Remember what goes around comes around. We can't all have the spotlight all the time. Encourage yourself to play the supporting role instead of the lead sometimes. Don't be a user, be a giver. It's not always about you. As a friend you need to strive to make it about someone else from time to time, too!

You get what you give

If you are not being a good friend, you will find that you do not have any good friends. You will always get what you give in this life. Good friends are wise. They will quickly recognize when all you do is take and never give. They will move on without you. They know that there is no shortage of good friends in the world. They have no problem heading out to find one to replace you with.

In order to have a good friend you must be willing to be a good friend. You must be willing to be selfless and dedicated to putting others first.

Remember there is no recession in Heaven. You cannot bankrupt the kingdom. If you find yourself feeling un-blessed, check your prayers. Are you asking for Good things? Are you praying bold prayers? Or are your prayers full of doubt and small expectations?

Your friend may be getting blessed better than you because she is praying better than you. Don't get jealous, get on her level. Start praying bold prayers. God wants you to be blessed not stressed, and certainly not jealous of the next. Don't get mad when your friends get their blessing.

Remember, what you wish for others is what you will get for yourself. In order to have a good friend you need to be a good friend.

Afterword

It is my prayer that you benefited from this book. I realize that not every section is pertinent to everyone. I hope that you were able to obtain what you were searching for and more inside these pages.

This book has talked all about getting rid of Frienemies/haters. It is extremely important to keep a good amount of space between you and the people who hate you. However, we do need haters. They are valuable motivators, but only from a distance.

When someone tells you what you can't do, says something negative about you or lives to make you feel defeated that is the person who should inspire you to do more in life! The key is that they shouldn't even know that they are motivating you.

Remember, not everything deserves a response. As a matter of fact, almost nothing people say about you deserves a response. The moral of the story is to let them think they won! What can you possibly gain from beating a hater at her own game? Let her win. Bow out gracefully. Then quietly climb to the top. Don't worry about making sure she sees your climb.

The haters are always lurking in the shadows watching your every move. Even after you cut all connections to them they are still sneaking in to take a peak. So trust me when I say they see you. They will see you win, but do it in a way that makes them feel as though you do not see them.

The most powerful thing you can do is cut a hater off and make them feel like you don't even remember their name. That's way more powerful than arguing with them (even when you're right and it's an easy case to prove). It's much more belittling to make a hater feel like they are too unimportant to even address.

That's how you win! That's how you fight a hater…by ignoring them. Going to great lengths to cut all ties is how you clear your pathway for good people to enter. You may not know it yet, but once you are surrounded by good people you won't even think about the hater you left behind.

It serves no benefit to you to address anything a hater does. Rest assured, initially when you ignore her she will increase the heat - but only because she wants some attention. Every time you bother to respond you are giving her the acknowledgement she wants. Remember, haters don't benefit you - you don't have the energy to respond to them.

No matter what they say, what they do, what they think…live your life without acknowledging their existence.

The good news is the world is full of women who are not insecure or jealous. And, once you have removed the negative squares out of your circle, you will be amazed how these great women will find you.

In life action follows thought. If you find a way to believe beyond what you see today and envision a life full of positive and true friends, they will indeed come to fruition in your life! There is no way around that.

Many people have a difficult time understanding the truth. The truth is the life you see is all a result of what you have created with your own thoughts. That's what your "point of view" is all about.

Start to dream out loud. Start to get a vision of good things in your future. You were not designed to go through this life alone. God wants you to be surrounded by friends who love and adore you. Get a vision of that.

No matter how you feel right now, envision your life in the future being perfect. Get a vision of you sitting around with a group of friends you can trust, ladies who you love and love you back, women who you share an abundance of laughs and good times with. Imagine being surrounded by females who are not jealous of you but are inspired by you. Get a picture of friends who are sincerely happy when you succeed.

The only thing stopping your dreams from becoming absolute reality is your own mind! That's it. It's like the old saying goes, whether you think you will or you think you won't – you are right! The first place we lose the battle is in our mind. Get a picture of yourself winning, and never lose it!

Your future is bright and full of the word "yes". It's your time whether you know it or not. You are about to feel a shift in your luck. Favor is with you, and it's going to stay. All you need to do is prepare your mind for the journey.

What are you willing to do to get the life you want? There are no Frienemies allowed in your future. You need to be prepared to separate yourself from them today in order to get what's in store for you tomorrow. Until you do you will remain stuck exactly where you are right now.

The first step is yours. Walk out on faith. Take a chance. The best is yet to come!

"When you like yourself, it is much easier to like other people." –Victoria Osteen

Regards,
Neisha

ABOUT THE AUTHOR

Neisha Robertson is a Professional Life Coach currently living in Houston, TX. Currently available for one-on-one counseling and life coaching sessions nationwide she has actively set out to change the world one person at a time. Through the group counseling sessions she hosts via Skype she is able to provide both advice and a listening ear for women. To join in visit her online at

www.authorneisharobertson.com.

Neisha is also available for speaking engagements, events, parties, book signings and book club hosting requests.

Bookings and inquiries can be made at:
AskNeisha@Gmail.com

Stay Connected:

https://twitter.com/DivasDramaGuide

www.facebook.com/authorneisharobertson

http://authorneisharobertson.com/

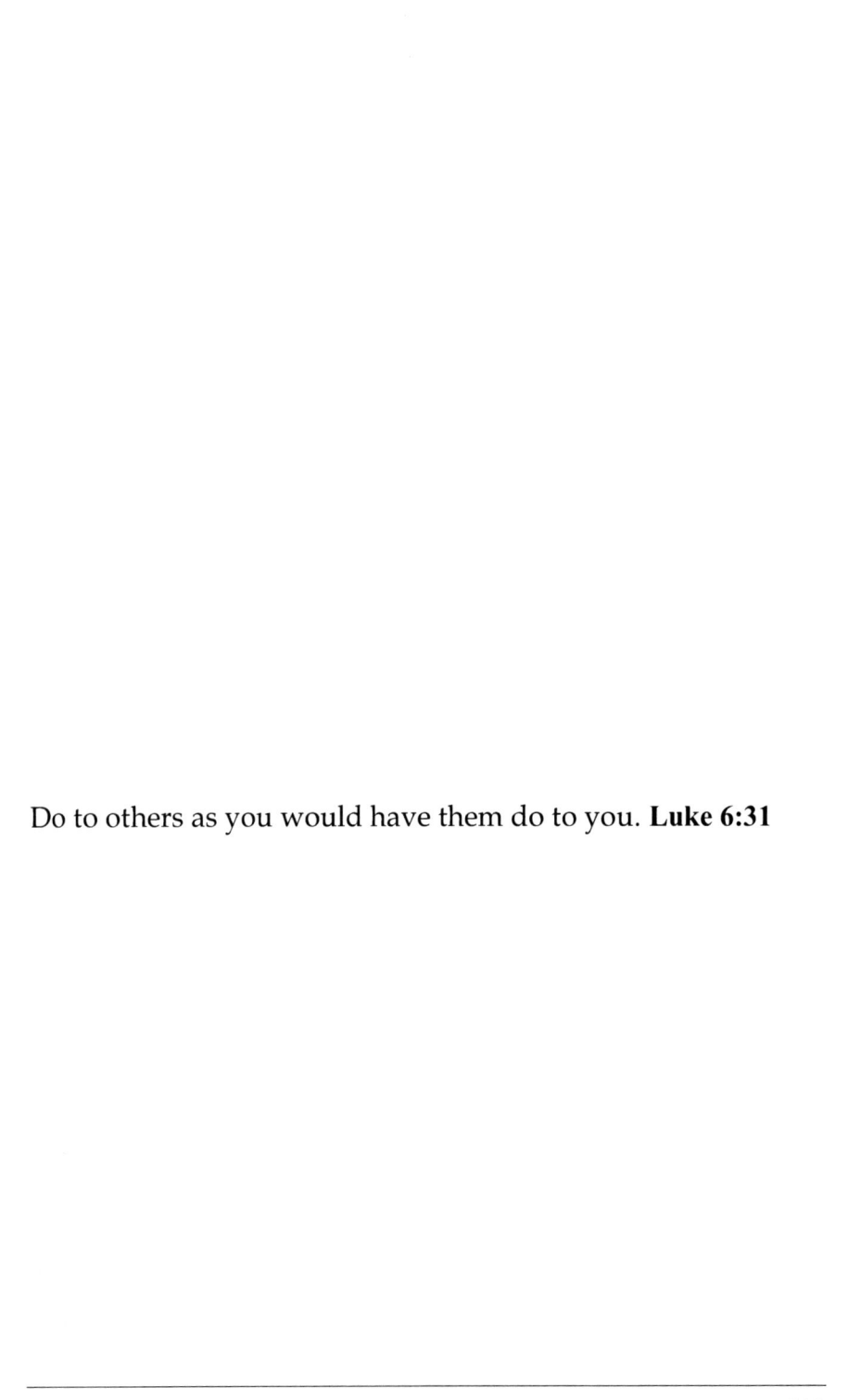

Do to others as you would have them do to you. **Luke 6:31**